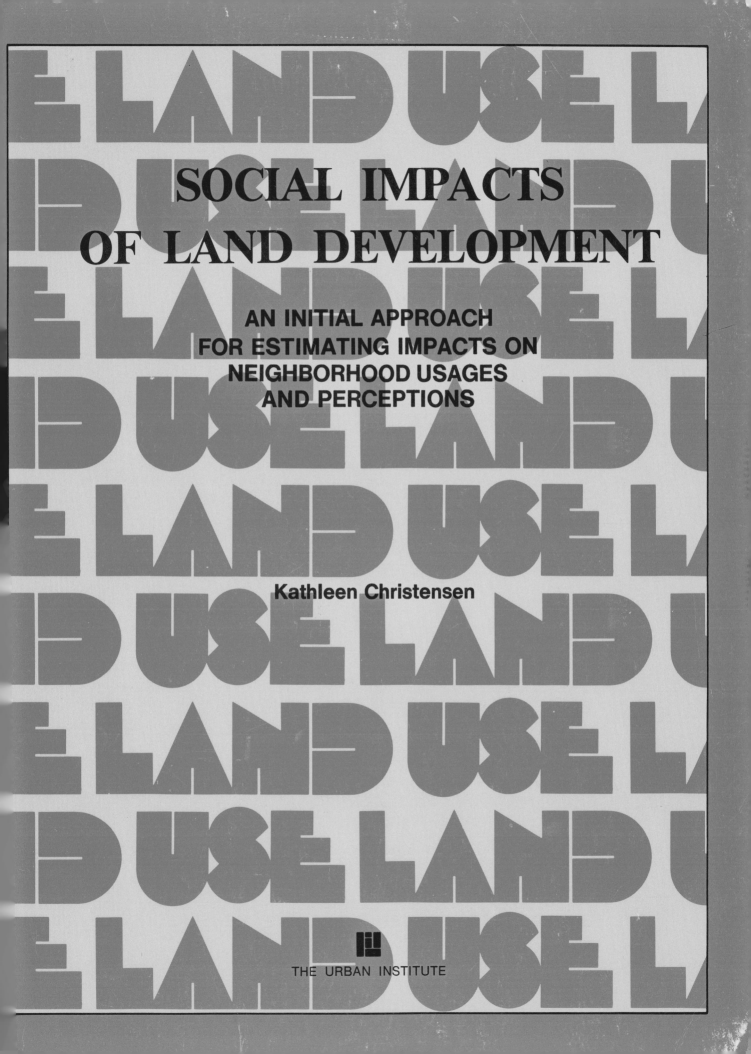

SOCIAL IMPACTS
OF LAND DEVELOPMENT

AN INITIAL APPROACH
FOR ESTIMATING IMPACTS ON
NEIGHBORHOOD USAGES
AND PERCEPTIONS

Kathleen Christensen

THE URBAN INSTITUTE

SOCIAL IMPACTS
OF LAND
DEVELOPMENT

AN INITIAL APPROACH
FOR ESTIMATING IMPACTS
ON NEIGHBORHOOD USAGES
AND PERCEPTIONS

Kathleen Christensen

The research for this report was made possible through a research grant from
the Office of Policy Development and Research of the U.S. Department of Housing
and Urban Development under the provisions of Section 701(b) of the Housing Act
of 1954, as amended, to The Urban Institute. The publication of this report
was supported by the Ford Foundation. The findings and conclusions presented
in this report do not represent official policy of the Department of Housing
and Urban Development, the Ford Foundation, or The Urban Institute.

THE URBAN INSTITUTE

Library of Congress Catalog Number 76-40755
U.I. 202-214-5
ISBN 87766-171-5

PLEASE REFER TO URI 15700 WHEN ORDERING

Available from:

Publications Office
The Urban Institute
2100 M Street, N.W.
Washington, D.C. 20037

List Price $3.95

Printed in the United States of America
First printing, September 1976

B/77/1M

TABLE OF CONTENTS

FOREWORD

The passage of the National Environmental Policy Act in 1969 prompted many local decisionmakers to better define and understand the impacts of land developments on their community. In response to their needs, many public and private research organizations focused their efforts on identifying the policy issues and methodologies relevant to impact evaluations. The Land Use Center of The Urban Institute has been actively involved in these efforts. Our impact evaluation series, of which this report is a part, has sought to clarify the economic, environmental and social effects of alternate land uses.

The first report of the series, Measuring Impacts of Land Development: An Initial Approach, established a series of impact measures that could be routinely used by local governments to assess the off-site effects of proposed land developments. This report also described various procedures for actually making the impact measurements. The final report in the series, Using An Impact Measurement System for Evaluating Land Development, reflects the insights gained after a year of studying the applicability of the measures to local land use decisionmaking processes.

A number of intervening reports have examined in detail the various effects which are likely to be associated with changes in the use of land. This study is concerned with how communities might consider the impact of a proposed development on the 'social character' of a neighborhood. The report describes techniques for determining whether new development will change the ways people use the outdoor public areas for recreation purposes; whether children will still have safe places to play; whether the elderly and others can walk to their grocery stores; and whether the residents still perceive

the neighborhood as a good place to live. Although many of the methods currently
available are in a very primitive stage of development, the report provides
a starting point for conducting social impact evaluations.

There is no simple answer to the question of whether a development should
be built. Opinions can be expected to vary widely. However, this report and
the others in this series should go some way to making those opinions better
informed.

ACKNOWLEDGMENTS

This study was sponsored by the Office of Policy Development and Research of the U.S. Department of Housing and Urban Development. It is part of a broader research effort by The Urban Institute Land Use Center on state and local evaluation of the impacts of land developments.

Worth Bateman, Executive Director of the Land Use Center, Philip Schaenman, Project Manager of this study, and Dale Keyes, Robert Sadacca, and Donald Fisk, all of The Urban Institute staff, provided valuable critiques and comments at various stages of this report. Jane Silverman edited the report and effectively contributed to its organization and content. The encouragement by James Hoben of the Division of Community Development and Management Research is also greatly appreciated.

Members of local planning departments and associated local agencies made significant contributions to this study. The thoughts and insights of Ross Vogelgesang, Director of the Division of Planning and Zoning, Indianapolis, Indiana, and Richard Tustian, Planning Director, Montgomery County, Maryland, are appreciated. Detailed technical discussions with Craig Kercheval and Gary Jursik of the Department of Metropolitan Development, Indianapolis, Indiana, and Earl DeBerge, Chairman, South Phoenix Planning Committee (a citizens' planning group), proved valuable.

Special thanks are also extended to Richard Counts, Zoning Administrator, Phoenix, Arizona; Mark Francis, planning consultant, Cambridge, Massachusetts; Roger Stough, City Planning Department of Baltimore, Maryland; and the members of our advisory group, for their valuable suggestions and critiques of drafts of this report.

ADVISORY GROUP

Timothy A. Barrow
Mayor
Phoenix, Arizona

Kurt W. Bauer
Executive Director
Southeast Wisconsin Regional Planning
  Commission
Waukesha, Wisconsin

Frank H. Beal
Director for Research
American Society of Planning Officials
Chicago, Illinois

Melvin L. Bergheim
Councilman
Alexandria, Virginia, and National League of
  Cities-U.S. Conference of Mayors

Richard F. Counts
Zoning Administrator
Planning Department
Phoenix, Arizona

Carl D. Gosline
Director of General Planning
East Central Florida Regional Planning
  Council
Winter Park, Florida

Bernard D. Gross
Planning Consultant
Washington, D.C.

Harry P. Hatry
Director
State and Local Government Research Program
The Urban Institute
Washington, D.C.

Ted Kolderie
Executive Director
Citizens League
Minneapolis, Minnesota

Denver Lindley, Jr.
Commissioner
Bucks County
Doylestown, Pennsylvania

Jack Linville, Jr.
Director, Land Management Program
Rice Center for Community Design and Research
Houston, Texas

Alan H. Magazine
Supervisor
Fairfax County Board
Fairfax, Virginia and Project Director
Contract Research Center
International City Management Association
Washington, D.C.

Robert H. Paslay
Planning Director
Planning Commission
Nashville, Tennessee

Richard A. Persico
Executive Director
Adirondack Park Agency
Ray Brook, New York

James R. Reid
Director
Office of Comprehensive Planning
Fairfax County, Virginia

E. Jack Schoop
Chief Planner
California Coastal Zone Conservation
  Commission
San Francisco, California

Duane L. Searles
Special Counsel on Growth and Environment
National Association of Home Builders
Washington, D.C.

Philip A. Stedfast
Planning Director
Department of City Planning
Norfolk, Virginia

David L. Talbott
Director of Planning
Falls Church, Virginia

Richard E. Tustian
Director of Planning
Maryland National Capital Parks and Planning
  Commission
Silver Spring, Maryland

F. Ross Vogelgesang
Director
Division of Planning and Zoning
Indianapolis, Indiana

Thornton K. Ware
Planning Director
Rensselaer County
Troy, New York

Joesph S. Wholey
Member
Arlington County Board
Arlington, Virginia, and Program Evaluation
  Studies Group
The Urban Institute
Washington, D.C.

Franklin C. Wood
Executive Director
Bucks County Planning Commission
Doylestown, Pennsylvania

SUMMARY

This report suggests an approach and data collection procedures to enable planners to estimate the social impacts of proposed land developments. It focuses on ways to estimate how proposed changes to the physical environment may affect citizens' uses and perceptions of their neighborhood. Its intended audience includes planners, appropriate line agency staff, and interested citizens who are involved in land use decisions that shape neighborhoods.

This is one of a series of Urban Institute reports on issues and methods relevant to estimating the fiscal, private economic, environmental, public service, and social impacts of proposed land development. The series is intended to encourage local governments to approach land use decisions in a more systematic and comprehensive way. The information generated should lead to better land use decisions, or at least to better understanding and communication of the effects of such decisions.

Scope of Report

The term "social" implies people living and interacting with other people. This report explores how the physical environment of a neighborhood may be changed by a proposed land development, and how these changes may affect the neighborhood as a social environment. The report focuses on seven areas of social impact that may be affected by changes in the physical environment:

1. recreation patterns at public facilities

2. recreational use of informal outdoor spaces

3. shopping opportunities

4. pedestrian dependency and mobility

5. perceived quality of the natural environment

6. personal safety and privacy

7. aesthetics and cultural values

These seven impact areas were selected because of their known relationship to the physical environment and to neighborhood satisfaction, and also
because it is possible to collect reasonably adequate empirical data on
citizens' perceptions and behaviors in each area. Impacts on elementary
schools, noise, and housing, which many also consider to be social impacts,
are discussed in other reports in this series. Discussion of additional
social impact areas, such as perceived friendliness or crowdedness, will not
be possible until additional work is done on developing procedures or estimating neighborhood social satisfaction.

The introduction of different socio-economic groups into a neighborhood can affect citizen satisfaction as much as changes in the physical
environment. This factor is not addressed in this report. However, the
framework of analysis outlined here might serve to answer some of the
impact questions in this sensitive and difficult area as well.

Before attempting to assess the social impacts of a project, planners
must answer three important questions. First, is the proposed development
significant enough to merit detailed evaluation, or can a more intuitive
evaluation suffice? Factors to consider in this decision include whether
the project will be precedent-setting as, for example, the first highrise
in a neighborhood of single-family detached homes, and what the anticipated
magnitude of the impacts will be.

Second, who will be impacted by the development? Social impacts will
be felt differently by groups. These groups may be defined in terms of
their proximity to the development; their socio-economic status; their roles
in the neighborhood; or their vested interest in the area. It is important
that impacts on clientele group(s) be disaggregated, so that major impacts
on a subset of citizens are not "averaged out" in communitywide statistics.

Third, what is the geographic boundary of the study area to be considered? This report suggests a method of analysis focused at the neighborhood level, residential neighborhoods in particular. The framework and techniques, however, could be applied to other types of neighborhoods, such as commercial areas. There are many ways to define a neighborhood, and no single choice seems best for all communities. It seems desirable that each community develop its own definition of neighborhoods as part of its comprehensive planning effort. Thereafter, specific land developments can be evaluated in light of their intra- or inter-neighborhood impacts.

Although this report focuses on the neighborhood level of analysis, planners and decision makers must look beyond the neighborhood and assess the impacts of a proposed project on the community at large. Often community-wide needs will differ. Decisions on a proposed project will result in a difficult trade-off between the two. These decisions are not easy to make. It is possible, however, for planners to approach the problem systematically and to gather the important facts on which to base their decision.

Though more and more local governments are recognizing the importance of social impact evaluation, many have been hampered by a lack of legal mandates that specifically require or allow the assessment of social impacts, and by a lack of funding and staff to undertake such assessments. Two other important constraints are lack of readily available or under- standable analytic approaches, and inadequate baseline data for detailing current social needs at the neighborhood level.

Steps for Estimating Social Impacts

The framework for estimating social impacts (outlined in Chapter 2) consists of five steps:

1. collect baseline data--profile current physical and social conditions in the neighborhood

2. identify physical changes to the neighborhood that will result with and without the development

3. estimate social impacts, or those differences between the "with development" and "without development" profiles

4. evaluate significance of the impacts

5. identify alternatives to mitigate the negative impacts

In developing a social impact analysis, it may not be necessary to devote equal attention to each step. Undoubtedly, the most critical and time-consuming step is collecting baseline data.

Methods for Collecting Baseline Data

Social science methodologies, such as citizen surveys, direct observation, and diaries, have been used by some local governments to collect baseline data on how citizens use and perceive of their neighborhood. Governments of all sizes can adapt these methods, and most can afford to use them. Baseline data are essential for estimating the neighborhoood impacts of a proposed development.

Citizen surveys can be used to collect data on what activities people engage in, where and how often the activities take place, as well as how people feel about specific places or conditions. Citizen surveys can be administered to a random sample of citizens in order to make generalizations about the population from which the sample is drawn. They can be administered by telephone, by mail, or in person, though the latter is preferable.

Direct observation can yield data on location and frequency of various outdoor activities. Direct observations can be made by a trained observer or sometimes by time-lapse photography.

Diaries are especially valuable for collecting detailed data on the exact sequencing of activities. Diaries can also be used to identify the type, location, and frequency of activities, especially when direct observation is awkward. Diaries are maintained by a sample of respondents, who bear the responsibility for recording specified types of data on their activities.

The baseline data can also be used for planning purposes, since they can help identify the needs for neighborhood residents and define development criteria or alternatives residents believe would be most responsive to their needs.

Recommendations

This study makes three tentative overall recommendations:

1. Local officials should consider the neighborhood impacts of all proposed land developments. Social impacts are of major concern to citizens, and existing data collection and analysis methodologies can be adapted for use by local governments. Detailed formal impact evaluations do not have to be completed on each proposed land development. However, all development proposals should be screened in light of a predefined set of impact measures that reflect potential impacts to neighborhood conditions. If warranted, a more detailed analysis of the proposed development can be conducted. An illustrative set of social impact measures is given in Exhibit 7. Suggested data collection and analysis procedures for these measures are given in Chapters 3 and 4.

2. Local officials should collect baseline data on citizen perceptions and uses of neighborhoods, especially those neighborhoods likely to have additional development in the short-to-medium run. These data can be used both for planning purposes and as a baseline in the review and evaluation of the impacts of proposed developments on citizen uses and perceptions of the neighborhood. A sample survey questionnaire is given in the appendix to this report.

3. <u>Local governments should assign responsibility for
    social impact data collection to one of their specific
    departments or divisions.</u> Unless there is such a group,
    the responsibility for such analyses may fall between
    traditional line departments.

1. INTRODUCTION

The scene: a public hearing on a proposed land development. Irate citizens, fearing for the fate of their neighborhood, passionately detail the social effects that a zoning, rezoning, variance, or site plan approval will have on their welfare. The local officials, zoning board members, and other decision makers who weigh these statements have few resources to support or refute the citizens' allegations or the challenges to them. This scene is played out thousands of times each year across the United States. Often citizen activists, rather than developers or local officials, flush out the social impacts of proposed projects. In order to avoid confrontations at public hearings, many local communities are stressing the importance of a legitimate social impact analysis process.

The term "social" implies people living and interacting with other people. Social impact analysis explores how a proposed land development can affect people living and interacting with one another. There are several approaches to social impact analysis, none of which alone provides the whole picture of how a development will affect social activities and needs.

Social impact analysis can be thought of further as the relationship between independent and dependent variables. A proposed land development may result in changes in one or more of several independent variables, such as the physical environment, the local economy, or the socio-economic characteristics of the population.[1] These changes, in turn, can affect any

---

1. For further discussion of how a land development can affect the economic structure of an area, see the other titles in this series, especially Thomas Muller, Fiscal Impacts of Land Development: A Critique of Methods and Review of Issues.

number of dependent social variables, such as recreation patterns, social cohesion, and rates of unemployment. Changes in all of these dependent variables can cause changes in how people interact. Exhibit 1 shows some of the possible relationships in social impact analysis.

This report is directed to the local planners, appropriate line agency staff, and activist citizens who are responsible for neighborhood land use decisions, and who attempt to assess systematically the social impacts of proposed projects. It does not attempt to present a system for weighting various impacts against each other. That process, always a difficult one, is a function of the goals and objectives of the neighborhood and the larger community. This report, however, develops a framework of analysis that helps clarify the way(s) social impacts can be analyzed.[2]

In recognition of the complexity of social impact analysis, this report has a narrow focus. Admittedly, this focus cannot include every social impact issue. Instead, the report explores how a proposed land development can change the physical environment of a neighborhood which supports human activities and interactions.

---

2. This report is one of a series of Urban Institute documents on issues and methods for measuring the fiscal, economic, environmental, public services, and social impacts of land development. Others in the series include Philip Schaenman and Thomas Muller, Measuring Impacts of Land Development; Thomas Muller, Fiscal Impacts of Land Development; Thomas Muller, Economic Impacts of Land Development; Dale L. Keyes, and Kathleen Christensen, Estimating Impacts of Land Development on Selected Services.

EXHIBIT 1

DETAILED IMPACT FLOW CHART

PROPOSED LAND DEVELOPMENT

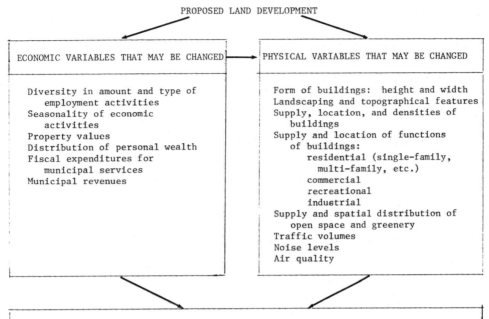

ECONOMIC VARIABLES THAT MAY BE CHANGED

Diversity in amount and type of
  employment activities
Seasonality of economic
  activities
Property values
Distribution of personal wealth
Fiscal expenditures for
  municipal services
Municipal revenues

PHYSICAL VARIABLES THAT MAY BE CHANGED

Form of buildings: height and width
Landscaping and topographical features
Supply, location, and densities of
  buildings
Supply and location of functions
  of buildings:
    residential (single-family,
      multi-family, etc.)
    commercial
    recreational
    industrial
Supply and spatial distribution of
  open space and greenery
Traffic volumes
Noise levels
Air quality

SOCIAL VARIABLES THAT MAY BE CHANGED

At Community Scale

Demographic Characteristics
  age, sex characteristics
  migration characteristics
  displacement of residents
  racial, ethnic characteristics

Institutional Membership
  civic groups
  religious groups
  social clubs
  political groups

Residential Patterns
  supply and distribution of
    various housing types
  segregation of social, racial,
    ethnic or income groups

Uses and perceptions of services
  recreation
  shopping
  mass transit
  schools
  health care

Perceptions of environmental quality

Perceptions of personal safety and
  privacy

Political power
  membership in dominant decision-
    making groups
  elected officials

At Neighborhood Scale

Demographic Characteristics
  age, sex characteristics
  migration characteristics
  displacement of residents
  racial, ethnic characteristics

Uses and Perceptions of Services
  recreation
  shopping
  mass transit
  schools

Recreation uses and perceptions in
  informal space around home

Pedestrian Mobility

Perceptions of environmental
  quality

Perceptions of personal safety and
  privacy

Aesthetic preferences
  visual attractiveness
  view opportunities
  historical resources

The physical environment, as used in this report, means the configuration of man-made and natural elements. It includes not only physical structures, such as open space, buildings, and roads, but also noise levels and traffic volumes. The residents of a neighborhood impart social "meaning" to these physical areas through the ways they use their spaces, and the manner in which they perceive their spaces.

In order to explore the social effects of changes to the physical environment, seven critical social impact areas are considered in this report. All are partially dependent on the physical environment.

1. recreation patterns at public facilities

2. recreational use of informal outdoor spaces

3. shopping opportunities

4. pedestrian dependency and mobility

5. perceived quality of the natural environment

6. personal safety and privacy

7. aesthetic and cultural values

Each of these impact areas was selected because of its known relevance to the physical environment and to neighborhood satisfaction. (The decision was based on a review of existing literature on neighborhoods.) Another very important factor in the selection process was the feasibility of collecting adequate empirical data on citizens' perceptions and behaviors associated with each impact area. Admittedly, there are other factors (such as school location, noise, and housing stock) that represent changes to the physical environment and that are related to neighborhood satisfaction. They are discussed in other reports in this series.[3] Changes, in the physical

environment, can affect how citizens perceive and use their neighborhood.

For example, if a proposed development would remove the only grocery accessible

by foot in the neighborhood, what effect would this have on families without

cars, who rely on a convenience store within walking distance of their homes?

Social impact evaluation is a relatively new field for many local govern-

ments. Its use by communities has been hampered by lack of staff, funding,

and usable analytic approaches. The procedures for data collection and

analysis suggested in this report have been kept as simple and practical as

possible. Though large planning departments, with ample staff and money,

will be able to use the methodologies outlined here in their most sophisticated

form, smaller communities can also apply these methods in a more limited, but

still useful, way. Nevertheless, no approach--including the one suggested

here--can be taken as the definitive set of methods for social impact evalua-

tion. Many of the ideas presented here are a distillation of discussions

with local planning officials--representing such diverse areas as urban design,

citizen participation, zoning review, and land use planning. However, pro-

cedures and measures presented in later chapters have not been tried out as

a unified social impact evaluation approach in a local community.

Although this study concentrates on social impact at the neighborhood

scale, such impact cannot be viewed as an isolated phenomenon. Often changes

at the neighborhood level have important communitywide repercussions. For

example, the addition of residents to a neighborhood could affect the

---

3. For a discussion of housing impacts, see Muller, Fiscal Impacts
of Land Development. For a discussion of public services impact, including schools, see Schaenman, et. al., Estimating Impacts of Land Development
on Public Services. For a discussion of noise impact, see Keyes, Land Development and the Natural Environment.

localized demand for municipal services, housing and employment opportunities.[4]

On the other hand, the net addition of people to the neighborhood may represent only a redistribution of population and services on the community scale. When planners review a proposed development, they should not only assess the potential social impacts at the neighborhood level, but also consider whether these impacts might have broader community ramifications.

Previous work in social impact analysis also had indicated that changes to the socioeconomic characteristics of the population may affect how citizens perceive and use their neighborhood. This type of analysis is very different than the one outlined for this report, and will not be discussed here. However, this report might lead to a better preparedness to deal with those complex and sensitive issues. A good starting point would be to evaluate how such changes will affect the seven social impact areas. For example, are some groups unwanted in the neighborhoods because of the demand they might create for unwanted stores? Are other groups viewed as negative impacts because of their differences in outdoor activity patterns?

Constraints on Social Impact Analysis by Local Governments

Why have so few local governments implemented a formal process for systematically identifying and evaluating social impacts? A review of the literature, as well as extensive discussions with planning officials in Indianapolis, Indiana, Montgomery County, Maryland, and Phoenix, Arizona, cities that participated in the study of which this report is a part, have helped identify several constraints, including the following:

1. a lack of legal mandates that specifically require the consideration of social impacts or that clearly define what should be considered under this rubric

---

4. Muller, Fiscal Impacts of Land Development, and Schaenman, et. al., Estimating Impacts on Public Services.

2. a lack of funding and staff and other support necessary for social
    impact assessment

3. a lack of readily available or understandable analytical frameworks
    for the identification and measurement of social impacts

4. a lack of baseline data detailing current social needs at the
    neighborhood and community levels

Lack of Legal Mandates

The legal mandates that exist for impact evaluation are generally initiated
at the federal[5] and state[6] levels. Local governments rarely require detailed
or explicit impact analysis on projects either funded by themselves or re-
quiring approval by appropriate local zoning or line agencies.[7] Within the
existing legislation, the term "environment" often refers only to characteristics of the physical environment, including the consideration of aesthetic
impacts. Rarely, does state or federal legislation allow or require evaluation
of other social impacts. Even when the legislation applies to local governments, consideration of social impacts is rarely encouraged or required.

When social impacts are admissible considerations, the guidelines issued
under the legislation generally provide weak definitions of the term "social."
For example, one set of state guidelines included the following broad listing
of variables that could be considered in an impact study: " ... distribution
and density of people; noise pollution; tranquillity and any other pertinent
social consideration; cultural uniqueness and diversity; and aesthetics and
natural beauty."[8] There was no explanation of what the terms meant or how

5. Frederick R. Anderson, NEPA in the Courts.
6. K. Christensen, et. al., "State-Required Impact Evaluations of Land
Developments."
7. An exception is the California Environmental Quality Act.
8. An example of guidelines issued by many states with environmental
policy acts is: Montana Environmental Quality Council, Second Annual Report.

they should be considered. (This criticism, however, often applies to economic
and environmental impact areas as well.)

Some communities do allow social impacts to be considered during zoning,
rezoning, or variance decisions. In evaluating a proposed project, for
example, the Montgomery County, Maryland citizens' guide to zoning directs the
County Council to consider "... the character of the neighborhood, (and) ...
its (development) impact on adjacent properties and the surrounding neighborhood..."[9] Neighborhood character rarely, however, is operationally defined
by the government.

Some local governments are establishing design and site review boards
for aesthetic review and regulation of proposed land developments.[10] A model
ordinance has been developed to incorporate visual concerns into the aesthetic
review process.[11] The legal basis for this type of aesthetic evaluation stems
from police powers.[12] Because of the difficulties in assessing the aesthetic
quality of each development, some jurisdictions have attempted to develop
explicit review standards and criteria for use in determining how a proposed
development will fit into the existing environment. The review is usually
limited to specific characteristics that can cause visual blight, such as
power lines, utility structures, or commercial and street signs. A detailed

9. Montgomery County Planning Board, Everything You Always Wanted to Know
About Planning, Zoning, and Subdivision in Montgomery County, Maryland
(October 1973).
10. Donald Ashmanskus, "Design and Site Review Boards: Aesthetic Controls
in Local Government," Management Information Service Report.
11. Carl Lindbloom, Environmental Design Review.
12. William Agnor, "Beauty Begins a Comeback: Aesthetic Considerations
in Zoning," Journal of Public Law, pp. 266-284.

impact evaluation is rarely prepared; often the site plan specifications provide the basis for the project review.

Inadequate Funding and Staff

At the local level consideration of how physical factors relate to social impacts usually occurs at the zoning, rezoning, or site plan review stages.[13] Although environmental and traffic implications of proposals are often presented at public hearings, the relevant social variables discussed in this report are rarely brought out. Because there is no explicit legal mandate, staff trained to do social impact analysis is not hired; because there is no staff funded to do the work, social impacts are not treated. The upshot is that few local planning departments, line agencies, or urban design divisions currently allocate budget or manpower for social impact evaluations, even though federal funds applicable to such studies do exist. (These include general revenue sharing money as well as funds from the Housing and Community Development Act of 1974).[14]

Many of the data collection approaches (such as surveys and direct observations) discussed in this report can be administered by individuals with little formal training in the social or behavioral sciences. Nevertheless, it is wise for planners without expertise in sampling procedures and survey data analysis to obtain expert advice in at least this area. Another alternative is to contract the work out to a local consulting firm or nearby university. If a consultant or university is used, local governmental staff

13. Michael Mandel, "The Various Legal Frameworks for Utilizing Impact Measures in Land Use Decision Making."
14. For further discussion, see Donald Gatton, David Garrison, and Richard Eckfield, "Community Development Block Grants: Action Steps for Local Government," Management Information Service Report, vol. 7, no. 1 Washington, D.C.: International City Management Association, January 1975.

members should either monitor or work with the outside advisor in order to help
ensure that the local government gets the kind of data it needs and that the
objectives of the study are met. Such a working relationship also orients
the local staff to the processes of data collection and analysis. If the
community later decides to undertake further studies, the local staff can
conduct them. This is especially important when academic resources are used,
because the commitment to the project may last only the length of the academic
year.

Lack of Analytical Framework

Although some federal agencies or academic bodies have conducted social
impact studies,[15] their research is generally not well known by local governments. Even when the studies are available, they are sometimes so riddled with
jargon that they are of little use to local officials. Furthermore, few
localities have the staff available to evaluate social impact methodology and
to develop their own appropriate frameworks of analysis.

Unavailability of Baseline Data

Planning departments generally consider the social needs of citizens
in the context of preparing a comprehensive plan or a functionally specific
program for, say, public housing or recreation. If the information gathered
details how citizens use and perceive of their neighborhoods, it may provide
the essential baseline data for social impact evaluation at the site plan or
zoning review stages of land use decisions. More often, however, social impact

---

15. For some of the better neighborhood social impact studies or reviews,
listed in the bibliography under Case Studies, see: Jon Burkhardt, "Neighborhood Social Interaction";
    Marshall Kaplan, Gans and Kahn, Social Characteristics of Neighborhoods
as Indicators of Effects of Highway Improvements;
    Donald Appleyard and Francis Carp, The Bart Residential Impact Study;
    U.S. Department of Transportation, Social and Economic Effects of Highways;
    U.S. Army Corps of Engineers, Social Impact Assessment: An Analytical
Bibliography.

information gathered by planning departments in the course of overall pro-
gramming for the community fails to filter down to the day-to-day project
review decisions.

Some local governments and citizen groups have sponsored studies of
citizens' activities and perceptions of their communities.[16] These broad
studies, however, are rarely incorporated into daily decisions of proposed
projects. As one reviewer of the urban design studies commented:

"Regrettably, the environmental quality concern may disappear at the
end of a single study because few of these cities have viewed environmental
design as a permanent function. Thus the studies often leave a legacy of
several small-scale projects or changes in zoning ordinances and master plans
but no one to implement them from environmental quality viewpoints."[17]

Detailed baseline data describing how individuals currently use and perceive places and conditions within their neighborhoods are critical to analyzing
social impacts. These data might best be collected as part of land use planning,
line agency service, or program evaluation, since there is considerable overlap

---

16. The City Planning Department of Baltimore, Maryland is currently
involved in a post-construction evaluation and planning effort for inner-
city parks. The department is studying citizen perceptions and uses of the
parks in an attempt to better design and manage public open space to meet
the needs of users. For further details, see Sidney Brower, "Recreational
Uses of Space: An Inner City Case Study," in Man-Environment Interactions.
    See also: San Francisco, California, City Planning Department, Social
Reconnaissance 1970 and Street Livability Study 1970 (1970); and
    Michael and Susan Southworth, "Environmental Quality in Cities and
Regions," Town Planning. This article focuses on urban design efforts.
    San Francisco Planning and Urban Renewal Association (SPUR), Impact of
Intensive High Rise Development in San Francisco. This feasibility study dis-
cusses methodologies for estimating impacts of highrise development on the
activities of the residents in surrounding neighborhoods, parks and plazas.
    17. Southworth and Southworth, "Environmental Quality in Cities and
Regions."

in data needed for these purposes. The information can then be used to
identify development goals in accord with the expressed needs of the citizenry.

If the meaning of social impacts is clarified and if data collection and
analysis are simplified, decision makers may feel more comfortable about getting
involved in this important type of analysis.

Chapter 2 suggests a working framework that can be used for evaluating the
social impacts of land developments and that can also be adapted for neighborhood planning purposes. Chapter 3 examines methodologies that can be used
to estimate impacts. Chapter 4 details specific problems in collecting data
for the seven critical social impact areas.

2. TOWARD A FRAMEWORK FOR MEASURING SOCIAL IMPACTS

We view our neighborhood environment on many levels, but two are of special importance for understanding social impacts. On one level, our neighborhood consists of objects, such as trees, streets, and buildings. On another level is our perception of these objects and the activities we associate with them.

In its physical manifestation, we all view a building as such, but we may each invest it with a different meaning. Similarly, we may perceive differently the impact of changes on our physical environment, depending on factors such as age and amount of time we spend in the neighborhood.

For example, suppose there were an abandoned building in a neighborhood that a developer proposed to replace with a new structure. Adults might view the building as an eyesore and a threat to the safety of their children. On the other hand, the children might perceive the building as a favorite play area: a haunted house full of mysteries and wonders. The removal of this object will have very different social impacts on these two groups.

Thus, among the three critical questions the planner must answer before assessing the social impacts of a proposed development is the question of which groups will be affected by the proposed project. Such groups can be identified in several ways. These include socio-demographic characteristics, proximity to the development, and household characteristics. Persons not currently living in the neighborhood, such as tourists or future generations, could also be affected by the proposed project. Clientele groups that might be affected by a project are listed in exhibit 2.

EXHIBIT 2

CLIENTELE GROUPS THAT MAY
BE AFFECTED BY A LAND DEVELOPMENT

(grouped by identifying characteristics)[1]

Socio-Demographic Characteristics

> Age groups
>
> Racial or ethnic groups
>
> Persons of various income groups

Household Characteristics

> Households in single-family units
>
> Households in multi-family units
>
> Households with children (x years and younger)
>
> Homeowners
>
> Home renters
>
> Long-time residents of neighborhood (x years and longer)

Role in Neighborhood

> Households
>
> Business owners
>
> Workers

Proximity to Proposed Development

> Living on site of proposed structure
>
> Living in neighborhood adjacent to proposed structure
>
> Other in community who do not live in the neighborhood but who may have special interest in it

Special Interests

> Tourists
>
> Users of specific facilities
>
> Future generations

---

1. Clientele groups can be variations or hybrids of the ones listed in this exhibit, e.g., one group might be neighborhood residents who have lived in the neighborhood 25 years or longer; another might be black homeowners with young children.

A second question that should be asked before undertaking a social impact
analysis is whether the development warrants a detailed evaluation. One
criterion might be the precedent-setting nature of the proposal, another,
the magnitude of the anticipated impacts. For example, the first highrise
structure in a neighborhood of single-family residences might set a precedent
that could result in major social impacts. A new highrise in a neighborhood
of apartment buildings may not appear to set much precedent, but if it removes
the only open space in the neighborhood, its social impact could be major.
Such a project would appear to be a good choice for closer scrutiny of its
social impact.

The third question is what is the geographic boundary of the study area
to be considered in the analysis? This report suggests a method of analysis
focused at the neighborhood level, particularly residential neighborhoods.
(The framework of analysis and the data collection methods could work equally
well, however, in commercial or mixed land use areas). Neighborhoods can be
defined and bounded in many ways: by man-made barriers, such as highways or
railroad tracks; by natural barriers, such as rivers or forests; by political
boundaries, such as census tracts or school districts; by easily discernible
land use characteristics, such as industrial or residential; or by unique
socioeconomic demographic characteristics of the residents, such as ethnic
groups.[18] No single definition will work for all communities. If each community
developed its own working definition, they could perhaps, as part of their
comprehensive plan, delineate the boundaries of neighborhoods in the developed

---

18. See American Society of Planning Officials, Neighborhood Boundaries,
PAS Report no. 141 (Chicago: American Society of Planning Officials, 1960);
and Terrence Lee, "Urban Neighborhood as a Socio-Spatial Scheme."

and developing parts of their jurisdiction. Thereafter, specific land development proposals could be evaluated in light of their inter- and/or intra-neighborhood impacts. It is important that these neighborhood boundary decisions be made prior to specific development proposals, so that the later identification of impacts will not be biased by dealing with too small or too large a geographic area.

Once the foregoing three questions have been answered, the planners can begin their analysis of the social impacts of a given project proposal. The rest of this chapter sets up a potential framework they can use in this evaluation.

Preparing a Neighborhood Social Impact Evaluation

There are five stages in preparing social impact evaluations:

1. collect baseline data--profile current physical and social conditions in the neighborhood

2. identify physical changes to the neighborhood that will result with and without the development

3. estimate social impacts, or those differences between the "with development" and "without development" profiles

4. evaluate significance of the impacts

5. identify alternatives to mitigate the negative impacts

Profile Current Conditions

All social impact evaluations need certain baseline data about the neighborhood to be affected: (1) the current physical and demographic characteristics; (2) the rates of change in those characteristics; and (3) citizens' uses and perceptions of the area. Exhibits 3 and 4 list variables that can be used to develop a baseline neighborhood profile. These types of data might best be collected annually as part of a planning, line service, or program

EXHIBIT 3

SAMPLE BASELINE DATA VARIABLES: PHYSICAL ENVIRONMENT OF
A RESIDENTIAL NEIGHBORHOOD

Housing stock

> Number of units by type (e.g., single-family, multi-family)
> Location (on map)

Open space (lot-size or larger)

> Type (e.g., publicly or privately accessible; wooded or high grass)
> Amount (number of acres)
> Location (on map)

Recreational facilities

> Number of units by type (e.g., playgrounds)
> Location (on map)

Shopping facilities

> Type (e.g., regional shopping center, convenience grocery store)
> Location (on map)

Landscaping

> Approximate type and amount of landscaping (e.g., tree-lined streets)
> Qualitative assessment

Traffic volumes

> On designated and sampled streets

Noise levels

> In decibels, from selected locations

Air quality

Crime rates

Street cleanliness

Cultural assets

> Inventory of sites or structures of historical, cultural, or scientific
> significance

EXHIBIT 4

SAMPLE BASELINE DATA VARIABLES: SOCIAL ENVIRONMENT OF
A RESIDENTIAL NEIGHBORHOOD

Demographic profile

> Age distribution
> Racial and ethnic distribution
> Income
> Education

Profile of neighborhood uses

> Recreation patterns at public facilities

>> Facilities used by households
>> Frequency of use
>> Type of users: by age, sex, and ethnic/racial groups

> Recreation patterns in informal outdoor areas (streets, sidewalks, open areas)

>> Areas used for activities (e.g., playing, socializing, exercising)
>> Frequency of use
>> Type of users: by age, sex, and racial/ethnic groups

> Shopping patterns

>> Stores and commercial groupings (identified by type or location) used by households
>> Frequency of users: by age and race

Profile of neighborhood perceptions[1]

> Environmental quality

>> Satisfaction with air quality
>> Satisfaction with noise levels

> Personal safety and welfare

>> Perceived safety from crime
>> Perceived safety from traffic
>> Satisfaction with privacy in exterior spaces around the home

---

1. Reasons for dissatisfaction should be collected for each item.

(Exhibit 4 -Continued)

Neighborhood aesthetics

    Overall attractiveness
    Identification of visually attractive places or features
    Identification of visually unattractive places or features
    Satisfaction with view opportunities from home
    Satisfaction with landscaping
    Satisfaction with maintenance and cleanliness of streets, sidewalks, and yards

Recreation opportunities

    Satisfaction with public and informal recreation opportunities
    Additional types of facilities desired

Shopping opportunities

    Types of additional stores preferred for the area
    Types of stores unwanted in the area
    Satisfaction with location of grocery stores

Satisfaction with school location

Satisfaction with mass transit opportunities

Profile of neighborhood pedestrian mobility

Number of households without automobiles

Number of households relying on pedestrian mobility to

    Grocery stores
    Recreation facilities
    Other relevant destinations

Overall neighborhood satisfaction

evaluation program. The direction and trends of change could then be plotted. A combined data collecting effort to get comprehensive baseline data on a specific neighborhood for both planning and project review purposes may provide economies. Some of the data generated, however, may not have immediate relevance to the specific projects under evaluation.

To do simply a "quickie" estimate of specific types of anticipated impacts from a proposed development, the procedures and sampling techniques can be simplified and modified. For example, if a development is going to remove a neighborhood convenience grocery store, the staff may want to collect data only on how often citizens use the store, available alternatives, and transportation available to other stores. However, a quickie survey has potential short-comings. If, for example, data on aesthetic and cultural values are collected as part of a more comprehensive plan, the data may show that the citizens rank the store as a treasured neighborhood landmark, and that its destruction will constitute a loss of more than just a shopping convenience.

Identify Physical Changes to the Neighborhood

This stage requires identifying changes to the physical conditions of the neighborhood (1) if the proposed development is built; and (2) if it is not built. Initial changes worth identifying might include the following:

1. Changes in the heights of buildings which might obstruct existing views and modify the extent and nature of shadow. From a community-wide perspective such changes could alter the physical profile of the town or city

2. the construction of a building which might remove open space, affect the physical appearance of the area; remove a buffer; or add shopping, recreational, or housing opportunities

3. removal of structures of architectural, historical, or cultural significance. Such removals generate a series of impacts, such as disruption of shopping patterns or neighborhood image

4. changes in traffic volumes, which might indirectly affect the design of streets and other circulation routes. Traffic volumes can also affect air quality and noise levels

5. change in noise levels, which might result from functional characteristics of such developments as a factory or a swimming pool

Some of these changes can be readily identified through information provided in the site plans. Others, such as noise, air quality, and traffic volumes, are harder to estimate. Exhibit 5 lists changes to the physical environment that may affect citizens' uses and perceptions of their neighborhood.

Once assembled, the data on the potential physical changes can be compared to expectations if the development is not approved.

Estimate Social Impacts--Methodological Approach

Exhibit 6 suggests ways to measure social impacts of the physical changes resulting from development. In rare cases, planners may be able to estimate accurately how changes in the environment will affect citizens' satisfaction with their neighborhood.

Usually, however, planners cannot estimate changes in satisfaction, because they do not know (1) exactly which physical conditions affect satisfaction the most; or (2) how much physical changes will cause citizens' satisfaction to change. The use of proxy measures is based on the assumption that certain conditions are related to satisfaction, and that citizens' expressed perceptions accurately reflect their feelings. Most of the proxy measures in exhibit 6 can be used to evaluate impacts of proposed development. Some, such as those on use patterns, can be used only in retrospective studies. We generally cannot predict how citizen uses of facilities or outdoor settings will change, except perhaps at the most general level, as when a facility such as a community swimming pool is removed.

EXHIBIT 5

SAMPLE APPROACH FOR DESCRIBING CHANGES
TO THE PHYSICAL ENVIRONMENT
(Columns 1 and 2 are not on a one-to-one correspondence)

Initial Changes	Secondary Changes (Where Relevant)[1]
Heights of buildings	Number of existing households whose exterior spaces will be overlooked because of the creation of new sightlines
Construction of a building on developed or undeveloped land	
Removal of existing structures	Number of households whose views are blocked, degraded, or removed
Traffic volume[2]	Location and type of areas that will be in shadow
Function of buildings	Amount, location, and type (e.g., corner lot or neighborhood park) of open space
Form and landscaping of proposed structures as compared to existing landscaping and design	Noise levels
	Air quality
	Number of residential structures removed
	Number and location of activity centers (e.g., stores, recreational facilities, schools, meeting halls)
	Number of structures of historical, cultural, or architectural significance

1. Many of the secondary changes can result from a variety of initial changes to the physical environment.

2. Some might consider this a secondary change.

EXHIBIT 6

SUMMARY OF NEIGHBORHOOD IMPACT MEASURES
AND BASELINE DATA REQUIREMENTS

Variables	Proxy Measures	Baseline Data for Measures	Possible Sources of Existing Baseline Data	Method for Collecting New Baseline Data

Socio-demographic characteristics of residents	Number and type of households displaced by development	Household sizes
		Number of years in residence
		Number of years in neighborhood
		Age distribution of residents
		  number and ages of children
		  number of residents over 65 years
		  of age
		Racial and ethnic groups
		Income distribution
			Census data (by the census block)	Citizen survey
				Citizen survey
				Citizen survey
				Citizen survey

Recreation at public facilities	Change in number or percent of households with access within x minutes of recreation facilities	Inventory of existing facilities by: type of facility, location, private versus public	Local department of parks and recreation	Walking survey of neighborhood
	Change in other physical conditions affecting households' current expressed satisfaction with recreation opportunities at public facilities, and number of households potentially affected	Perceptions of the facilities in terms of overall satisfaction with the opportunities facilities they feel are needed undesirable facilities factors contributing to dissatisfaction	Survey conducted for recreation department	Citizen survey
	Change in number or percentage of households using facility, by type of facility, and frequency of use	Usage patterns in terms of: who uses facilities frequency of use	Attendance records of facility	Citizen survey
Recreation in informal spaces around the home	Change in availability of physical settings that x number of people currently used for recreation activities	Inventory of outdoor settings used for activities		Direct observation citizen survey, diary, traffic counts
	Change in other physical conditions affecting households' current expressed satisfaction with recreation opportunities in informal spaces around home, and number of households potentially affected	Usage patterns, in terms of: activities in each setting who uses the settings frequency of use		Direct observation, citizen survey, diary
		Existing traffic volumes on selected streets at selected times		Traffic counts
		Perceptions of the settings in terms of: satisfaction with opportunities factors contributing to dissatisfaction		
Shopping	Change in number or percentage of households within x minutes of desired shopping facility	Inventory of existing stores: by type by location	Chamber of Commerce (for specific area)	Driving/walking survey
	Change in number or percentage of households using facility by type of facility and frequency of use	Perceptions of shopping opportunities, in terms of: types of stores desired undesirable types of stores satisfaction with shopping opportunities factors contributing to dissatisfaction		Citizen survey

EXHIBIT 6 - Continued

	Change in other physical conditions affecting household current expressed satisfaction with neighborhood shopping opportunities and number of households potentially affected	Usage patterns in terms of: who uses stores / frequency of use — Citizen survey on site users
Mass transit	Change in number or percentage of households within x minutes of transit stops / Changes in scheduling or routing affecting household' current expressed satisfaction with mass transit opportunities, and number of households likely to be affected	Inventory of existing mass transit opportunities, in terms of: stops / route destinations — Driving/walking, Mass transit agency / Perceptions of the adequacy of mass transit opportunities: overall satisfaction / factors contributing to dissatisfaction — Citizen survey
	Change in number or percentage of households using mass transit, by frequency of use	Usage patterns in terms of: who uses system / frequency of use — Citizen survey
School location	Change in number or percentage of households within x minutes of school locations / Change in other physical conditions affecting current expressed satisfaction with school location, and number of households potentially affected	Inventory of existing school locations — School board / Perceptions of: satisfaction with location / factors contributiong to dissatisfaction — Citizen survey
Pedestrian mobility	Change in physical conditions affecting households' current expressed satisfaction with walking conditions and number of households potentially affected / Change in number or percentage of households able to walk within x minutes to desired destination, e.g., stores, recreation facility, transit stops, school	Street layout: location and width of streets / Sidewalks: location / Traffic volumes on selected streets at selected times of day — County and city engineers, Traffic counts / Number of automobiles per household / Number of households relying on walking mobility to such destinations as: stores / recreation facilities / schools / mass transit stops — Census data, Citizen survey / Perceptions of walking conditions, in terms of: satisfaction / factors contributiong to dissatisfaction — Citizen survey, Survey of users at site, Survey of owners, managers, or principals, Citizen survey
Perceived environmental quality	Change in specific physical conditions affecting households' current expressed satisfaction with perceptible characteristics of air quality (e.g., smoke plumes, odor) and number of households potentially affected / Change in specific physical conditions affecting households' current expressed satisfaction with characteristics of noise levels, and number of households potentially affected.	Selected measure of ambient air quality — Environmental quality department / Identification of smoke plumes or odors — Visual inspection / Perceptions of air quality, in terms of: satisfaction / factors that contribute to dissatisfaction — Transcripts of public hearings, Citizen survey / Selected measure of noise levels — Noise meters / Perceptions of noise quality, in terms of: satisfaction / factors contributing to dissatisfaction — Transcripts of public hearings, Citizen survey

EXHIBIT 6 - Continued

Criterion	Measure	Effect	Source / Organization	Data collection method
Perceived personal safety and privacy	Change in traffic volumes and other conditions affecting households' current expressed satisfaction with physical safety from traffic and number of households potentially affected	Traffic volumes		Traffic counts
	Change in physical conditions affecting households' current expressed satisfaction with security from crime and number of households potentially affected	Crime rates		Telephone survey
	Identification of features of the proposed development that may be harmful to children, and number of children potentially affected	Natural or man-made hazards, e.g. stone quarries, open construction sites	Engineering department	Walking/driving survey or citizen survey
	Change in sightlines, pedestrian volume, or other conditions that affect households' current expressed satisfaction with privacy and number of households potentially affected	Heights of surrounding structures	Police department	Visual inspection
		Perceptions of security, in terms of: feelings of safety, factors affecting insecurity		Citizen survey
		Perceptions of privacy in terms of: satisfaction with privacy in outdoor areas, factors affecting dissatisfaction		Citizen survey
Aesthetics and cultural values	Change in physical conditions of neighborhoods that are currently rated as physically attractive	Rating of overall attractiveness		Citizen survey
	Number of households whose view opportunities are blocked, degraded or improved	Identification of visually attractive places or conditions		Citizen survey
	Perceived importance of landmarks to be lost or made inaccessible or accessible	Identification of visually unattractive places or conditions		Citizen survey
		View opportunities, in terms of: number of households with view opportunities, satisfaction with views, factors affecting dissatisfaction		Geometric analysis and citizen survey
		Perceptions of maintenance and upkeep of: streets and sidewalks, yards, exteriors of buildings		Citizen survey
		Inventory of cultural or historical landmarks	Local or state historical societies	
Overall satisfaction with neighborhood	Change in number or percentage of households satisfied with their neighborhood	Perceived overall satisfaction		Citizen survey
		Perceived neighborhood improvements		Citizen survey
		Identification of unique places in neighborhood		
Sociability	Addition or removal of gathering places, e.g., meeting halls, churches (See Recreation at Public Facilities and Outdoor Informal Spaces for other possible proxy measures)	Inventory of existing gathering places	Civic groups	Walking survey
		Identification of use	Neighborhood groups	Citizen survey

Planners can use two approaches when relying on proxy measures for evaluating proposed development: qualitative inference and comparative studies.

<u>Qualitative Inference</u>: This involves a case study description of one neighborhood and an identification of possible physical changes the development will engender. Included would be existing physical design layout, and environmental conditions; the demographic characteristics of its residents; and citizen uses and perceptions. Impacts are estimated by inferring how the changes to the physical environment will affect citizen uses and perceptions. Inference involves judgmental estimates of how satisfaction levels and activities will change when specific neighborhood places are altered.

Although inference appears to be one of the most practical social impact approaches available to planners, it has obvious limitations. There is always the possibility of making an erroneous speculation based on limited data or unusual circumstances. The reliability of inferences can be partly checked by monitoring changes to the neighborhood after the development is completed to see how accurate the original forecasts were. For such an evaluation, a planning staff may want to do repeated case studies (by surveys, direct observations, etc.) of random samples of the same population to see how perceptions and activities have changed. Surveys called longitudinal studies can also be administered at intervals to the same sample. Such validation is time-consuming and expensive, and is rarely done in local governments today.

<u>Comparative Studies</u>: An alternative approach for estimating impacts is to compare two neighborhoods at the same time--one where a project is proposed, the other, where a similar project has already been completed. The two projects and neighborhoods must be similar in size; project type, location, and design; socioeconomic factors; and geographic characteristics. The data sources for the two areas and projects should also be similar. Comparative surveys, for

example, can be used to collect data on citizen uses and perceptions to compare and relate differences to the changes in the physical environment brought about by the development.

The San Francisco Planning and Urban Renewal study of the impacts of intensive highrise developments on surrounding neighborhoods[19] used the comparative study approach to forecast how a change in the physical environment, such as a new highrise, would impact current activity patterns in lowrise neighborhoods. First, planners observed and recorded outdoor behaviors, such as children's play and informal adult gathering, on similar residential blocks--some with and some without highrise development. Then they assessed the differences in informal outdoor activities. Many of the differences were attributed to the changes brought about by the highrises.

Comparative studies entail a double effort for data collection and assume that a proposed project has an accessible twin. Even if similar circumstances can be found, the results may differ because of various random and nonrandom effects.

It would be preferable to compare the proposed project with several analogous cases to see what effects usually result. But it takes time and consistent effort (in terms of research design, sampling techniques, and survey instruments) to develop a useful collection of case studies.

Evaluate Significant Impacts

When planners evaluate which changes to the physical environment will cause significant social impacts, they are confronted with a difficult question: whose values and objectives should be used in the assessment? As already noted,

---

19. San Francisco Planning and Urban Renewal Association, "City and Neighborhood Character."

the decision maker must make an evaluation in light of both neighborhood perceptions of what is important and communitywide objectives. For example, a proposed highway might severely disrupt neighborhood activities and be viewed by local residents as a social cost. Yet the highway might be very important to the community at large to facilitate inter-neighborhood mobility and to relieve congestion. What may be a benefit at one scale can thus be a cost at another.

While these trade-offs are never easy to make, the planners who gather detailed information about the activities and perceptions of a neighborhood are in a position to come to a decision based on facts.

An important question planners must ask in estimating negative effects is how neighborhood households can (or would have to) adapt to the changes. Will they change their activities or perceptions to accommodate the change in the physical environment? For example, if traffic is increased on a street where children normally play, will the children walk the six blocks to the nearest park?

Another method of adapting to change is assimilation. Can the development be assimilated into the neighborhood so that current activities or perceptions are enhanced and preserved? For example, can the plaza of a new structure substitute for the informal park formerly used by the elderly and by mothers with small children?

This brings us to the last step of the evaluation process, which is to identify mitigation efforts that might offset negative effects.

Identify Alternatives to Mitigate Negative Impacts

Mitigation efforts are the design, locational, or functional features of the proposed development that can be changed to offset the development's anticipated negative impacts. Exhibit 7 shows examples of potential impacts and possible mitigation efforts. The planners' objective is to integrate a proposed development into the existing setting in a manner acceptable to the neighborhood households. Estimates of social impacts should be made with and without the mitigating factors, both to assess the alternatives and to explore possible long-range impacts of the development.

EXHIBIT 7

MITIGATING SOCIAL IMPACTS: AN EXAMPLE

Physical	Social Impact	Mitigation Effects
Creation of new sight-lines	Number of households with change in outdoor activities around the home, because of loss of privacy	Reposition windows to decrease number of households that will experience visual invasion; erect landscaping barrier
	Number of households perceiving loss of privacy	
Increased traffic volumes	Number of children whose play activities will be disrupted because of threat of traffic accident	Develop substitute park
	Number of households whose pedestrian mobility will be disrupted	Erect pedestrian bridge; place traffic lights where children cross busy intersections
Creation of auto junkyard (a nuisance)	Number of children whose physical safety will be threatened	Reduce visibility or access (e.g., high fence)

3. GENERAL PROCEDURES FOR ESTIMATING SOCIAL IMPACTS

There is no single best way to do a social impact evaluation. The types of impact areas and the data collection methodologies vary among developments, based upon the size, location, and function of the project, the nature of the neighborhood, the magnitude of expected impacts, and the staff time and funding capacities of the planners responsible for the evaluation. This chapter discusses the main data collection methods for carrying out social impact analysis and shows how they might be applied to a specific project.

An important aspect of these methods--their cost--is not discussed. Except in the case of surveys, for which cost comparisons are included, this information is unavailable.

Baseline Data Collection Methods

Exhibit 6 lists the suggested impact measures and summarizes the types of baseline data needed, as well as appropriate sources and methods. The citizen survey is the method most often suggested for gathering data on citizen perceptions; whereas direct observation, diaries, and citizen surveys are generally used to gather information on behavior. Each method can be adapted for project reviews as well as for planning purposes. The references cited in this chapter provide more detailed discussion of the data collection methods discussed.

Survey.[20] Surveys are the systematic collection of data from populations, or samples of populations, through direct contact with people by means of

---

20. For more detailed discussion, see National Bureau of the Standards. _User Requirements in the Home-Data Collection Methodology_; A. N. Oppenheim, _Questionnaire Design and Attitude Measurement_; Carol Weiss and Harry Hatry, _An Introduction to Sample Surveys for Government Managers_; William Michelson, _Behavioral Research Methods in Environmental Design_; Dennis Forcese and Stephen Richer, _Stages of Social Research: Contemporary Perspectives_ (Englewood Cliffs, New Jersey: Prentice Hall 1970); Matilda White Riley, _Sociological Research: A Case Approach vol. 1 and Exercise and Manuals_, (New York: Harcourt Brace and World, Inc., 1963.)

personal interviews, telephone, or mail. They are generally based on a scientifically selected sample, rather than the total population, because this is more economical. There are a number of considerations in the choice and development of a survey. First, will the survey yield the most appropriate information? Second, what type of population sample should be drawn, and what type of survey approach should be used? Third, how should the survey instrument be designed--what questions should be asked; how should they be phrased and sequenced; who should ask them; and should they be asked in person, over the phone, or by mail? Many of these points are briefly addressed in the following discussion.

Surveys are not especially helpful in providing information that requires extensive recall by the respondents. They may also be inadequate for use with specific clientele groups, such as small children. However, a properly designed and used survey can provide, at a reasonable cost, the most representative and comprehensive information on what people do and how they feel.

Types of Data Generated. Surveys can be used to gather three types of information: descriptive (e.g., how many people are in the family, how often do they use the public swimming pool), evaluative (e.g., how satisfied are they with recreational opportunities), and explanatory (e.g., what factors contribute to their dissatisfaction). In many circumstances, surveys are the only viable way to gather these data.

The appendix to this report presents a sample survey that can be adapted to meet the baseline data needs of a proposed project. In some instances, rather than use the full survey, planners will want to use "quickie" surveys with a few questions geared to a specific impact area, such as outdoor recreation patterns or shopping, to collect data quickly and cheaply on a particular project. If, however, a neighborhood is scheduled for rapid growth in the near future, a more comprehensive survey may prove beneficial so data can also be used in formulating other plans for the area.

Surveys can generate information on a number of persons and specific clientele groups, defined by area of residence or by socioeconomic and demographic characteristics such as age, income, number of children, age of children, and automobile ownership. These data can later be used in interpreting the variations in responses to survey questions. Alternatively, the sample can be stratified by clientele groups, to determine the perceptions and uses of each. Other sources, such as census records, may also be helpful in obtaining some of the information, but since the data are collected only at certain time intervals, there is rarely any indication of the current accuracy of the information.

Not only can a survey provide data that help to evaluate a given proposal, it can also be used to seek explanations for a respondent's feelings about a project or specific situation. The follow-up questions can often identify prescriptive courses of action.

Several techniques are currently available for measuring attitudes or perceptions. For purposes of standardization and comparison, the sample survey in the appendix relies on simple four- or five-point response scales. The respondent's attitude is directly inferred from the answer given, e.g., "very satisfied" versus "very dissatisfied." A number of references on attitude measurement scales are cited in this chapter and in the bibliography at the end of this report.[21]

---

21. Allan L. Edwards, Techniques of Attitude Scale Construction; L. L. Thurstone and Ernest Chave, The Measurement of Attitudes (Chicago, Illinois: University of Chicago Press, 1948).

Sampling Methods. A population is the total number of people or units to which the survey results apply. For example, in a neighborhood study, the population might be all households or business owners in the neighborhood. When undertaking a survey, the first question is generally whether to reach all members of the population or a selected sample. It is not necessarily better to survey everyone. A survey of 100 percent of the population is virtually impossible to carry out, and it is hard to weight individuals that the survey misses.

All types of sampling methods fall into one of two categories: probability and nonprobability samples. In a probability sample, each individual in the total population has a known probability of appearing in the sample. Generalization of sample results to the population can then be made, and the precision of estimates can be assessed. A very important concern is what sample size should be used. The choice usually depends on the accuracy desired, weighed against the costs of administering the survey.[22]

For each type of probability sample, a list of all members of the population must be compiled. This is called a sampling frame. Problems with probability sampling can occur if sampling frame is incomplete or inaccurate.

The most common type of probability sample is the simple random sample, where every person or unit in the population has an equal and independent chance of being selected. The second basic type is the stratified sample. This requires the grouping of members of the population into strata (homogeneous groups) by some identifying characteristics (such as family life cycle types:

---

22. See Weiss and Hatry, Introduction to Sample Surveys, for discussion of sample size and precision of estimates. Also useful are L. Festinger and D. Katz, eds., Research Methods in the Behavioral Sciences; and Hubert M. Blalock, Social Statistics.

married without children, married with children). A random sample is then selected from each stratum. Stratified samples ordinarily do not give every member of the total population the same chance of being selected, but they allow the comparison of subgroups whose numbers are too small to be covered adequately in a random sample of the entire population.[23]

Types of nonprobability samples include systematic and cluster sampling. Systematic sampling involves selection of respondents from the list of population at designated intervals after a random start in the first interval. For example, if the population is 2,000 and we want a sample of 100, the sampling interval would be 2000/100 = 20. A random number from 1 to 20 would then be selected, as would every twentieth number thereafter. This method is useful because it avoids detailed selection procedures, but it may introduce biases.

Cluster sampling is the least expensive method for very large-scale surveys. It involves selecting the population group, and then selecting clusters within clusters until the desired survey unit is reached. This method is useful when specific information about a given area or site plan arrangement is needed or when travel costs between interviews must be cut down; but it can yield fewer objective, independent samples.

Administration. The staff must decide how to adminster the survey. Will it be done in person, over the phone, or by mail?

Surveys by mail are generally the cheapest of the data collection methods. They are often used when the geographic area to be covered is large, when personal and possibly embarrassing questions are being asked, or when several members of a household are to respond individually to the questions. A

23. Hubert M. Blalock, An Introduction to Social Research.

disadvantage however is that the response rate is generally low (20 to 40 per-cent), compared to the high return on personal interviews (80 percent).[24] Respondents who return a mail-out survey also may differ significantly in terms of income, education, attitudes, and behaviors from people who do not return the questionnaire.

The telephone survey is gaining in popularity because of its relatively low cost compared to personal interviews and because a growing number of U.S. households now have telephones.[25] In some areas, however, a good proportion of the population such as the poor, may not have telephones.

The in-person interview is the most commonly used method for administer-ing surveys. It allows for clear instructions about answering questions. It ensures, as much as possible, a high return and completion of the questions, and also allows the local government to communicate with respondents in ways that are more satisfactory to them. However, it is the most expensive of the three. Relative costs are shown in exhibit 8.

Direct Observation.[26] Direct observation objectively records physical conditions and behaviors in specific settings. It can be used to collect data on what activities people engage in, how many engage in them, where the activities take place, and who the actors are, in terms of visible features such as age, sex, and race. Direct observations, unlike surveys, cannot question how satisfactory activities are, or why facilities are not used. But they can provide data on groups, such as small children and adolescents

24. Weiss and Hatry, Introduction to Sample Surveys.
25. J. C. Scott and Eliska Chanlett, Planning the Research Interview.
26. E. J. Webb, et. al., Unobstrusive Measures--Non-Reactive Research in the Social Sciences, (Chicago: Rand McNally, 1968); Robert Bales, Interaction Process Analysis, A Method for the Study of Small Groups, (Cambridge, Mass.: Addison Wesley Publishing Co., Inc., 1950); Riley, Sociological Research.

EXHIBIT 8

COMPARISON OF COST AND ACCURACY LEVELS
FOR DIFFERENT SAMPLE METHODS AND SIZES
(rough approximation for illustrative purposes)

SAMPLE METHODS AND SIZES	COST LEVEL[1]		ACCURACY LEVEL[2]	
			The total population would differ from the sample by the following percentage points for a confidence of:	
	Total	Approximate cost per response	95 percent	90 percent
Personal interview				
Sample of 400	$ 9,925	$24.80	± 4.9	± 4.1
Sample of 500	11,325	22.65	± 4.3	± 3.6
Sample of 1,000	19,550	19.55	± 3.1	± 2.6
Telephone interview				
Sample of 500 (including 50 in-person interviews)[3]	8,510	17.00	± 4.3	± 3.6
Mail questionnaire 2,000 mailed 1,000 returned (supplemented by 50 telephone and/or in-person interviews)	8,475	8.10	a	a

1. Costs are the estimated "moderate" costs in the appendix of Weiss and Hatry. They apply to the survey assumptions described there. The costs include both administration and analysis of the survey.

2. Accuracy levels are the percentage points (+ or -) by which the sample percentage could differ from the "true" percentage in the population, if the reported percentage is about 40 to 60. (They are obtained from exhibits 3 and 4 of Weiss and Hatry). Nonsampling errors are not considered here.

3. If all assumptions of randomization have been met.

a. Because of self-selective nature of returns, this difference will inevitably be greater than the earlier sampling tables indicate, but is very difficult to forecast how serious this bias is.

Source: Weiss and Hatry, Introduction to Sample Surveys.

that are generally underrepresented on surveys. In developing a neighborhood study on citizen perceptions and activity patterns, it is worthwhile to use diverse methods rather than to rely totally upon one.

Design Factors. Direct observations can be conducted in any sort of space where the planner needs to know the number of people engaged in various activities. One of the initial concerns is which sites will be observed. The selection of site(s) is based on what type of impacts are anticipated and what areas may be changed by the development. Activities occurring in parks, on sidewalks, on stoops or porches, and in the street are candidates for observation. In research carried out by the city of Baltimore,[27] the emphasis is on how people use inner-block parks, as compared to fronts of their houses.

The second concern is which activities in the area should be observed and recorded. Should observers tally all people on the streets, regardless of what they are doing, or should they limit their observations to people stand-ing, walking, or playing games? Precoded formats that specify the type of activities to be recorded (see exhibit 13, Chapter 4, for examples) facilitate the standardization and tabulation of data, but limit the types of activities to be identified and recorded. Such formats can be helpful in gathering data on the level of outdoor activity.

Among other factors that can affect activities in the area being observed the primary one is weather. If a direct observation is conducted on a rainy, cold day, the frequency of outdoor activities and number of participants will generally be less than if the observation were done on a pleasant spring day.

_____

27. Brower, "Recreational Uses of Space," Baltimore, Maryland, City Planning Department, Neighborhood Design Study.

Other factors are the times the observations are conducted, and the racial and personal characteristics of the observer. Is it better to use indigenous or "foreign" (i.e., alien to the area in terms of acquaintance, race, and age) observers? The Baltimore study previously cited was conducted in a black inner-city neighborhood. Observers were black neighborhood residents, so that the observations could be made without changing the phenomenon being studied. It is commonly felt that observers should be as inconspicuous as possible.

If planners wish to record the level of outdoor activity at peak or at average times, they should be selective as to when the observations are conducted. For example, if the prime concern is to identify how school-age children use places along the streets where traffic volumes will increase, it might be best to perform the observations on summer days. The planners should also select times that provide a representative sampling of the activities likely to occur. Observations can be conducted by stationing an observer at one place all day. The Baltimore study, however, used a "walking census," in which observers, on designated days and at specific times, walked through a neighborhood and systematically recorded, on a precoded format, activities happening ahead of and beside them.

Unless observations are distributed over a random sample of seasons, days, times of days, and climates, a representative overview of the type and frequency of activities in outdoor settings is hard to obtain. An alternative approach is to choose the season and days when there is thought to be the greatest diversity and frequency of outdoor activities.

In summary, when a proposed land development is going to disrupt severely the physical settings of a neighborhood, it may be advantageous to document the types and locations of activities, and the number and types of participants at specified places and times, so that losses can be identified and alternative settings selected. To complement this information, a survey can indicate the frequency of use, and offer insights on the importance people attach to places and their satisfaction with them.

Diary.[28] A time-activity diary is a log of the sequence and duration of activities engaged in by individuals over a specified period. It can be used for obtaining detailed information on specific activities: where they occur; other people engaging in the activities; and their duration. The researcher can also identify clusters of activities that occur in specified places. Diaries may also be useful in neighborhoods where an observer might be a conspicuous intruder. Diaries alone cannot yield reliable data.

Format. The format for collecting diary data can be precoded or open-ended. The precoded format (see exhibit 14, chapter 4) specifies which activities should be recorded. It makes the tasks of recording and analyzing the data somewhat easier. The open-ended format allows for freedom of response, but poses a problem in categorizing and tabulating the responses.[29]

Administration. The usual practice in administering a diary is to leave it with a respondent (preferably selected at random). The respondent should be clearly told how the information is to be recorded. It is important to specify the time frame in which the information should be recorded (e.g., for three weeks), the times information should be recorded, (e.g., every hour or every time an activity changes), and when the completed diary will be retrieved. The interviewer who picks up the completed diary can check the responses and request additional information on missing points.

---

28. William Michelson and Paul Reed, "The Time Budget," in Michelson, Behavioral Research Methods; National Bureau of Standards, User Requirements in the Home.
29. Michelson, op. cit.

If the researcher is interested in obtaining data about activities that occur infrequently, then respondents should record their activities over extended time frames. There should be continuing communication with the respondents to ensure that their motivation is kept high, and that they keep consistent and accurate diaries. In the Baltimore study, an interviewer arranged to pick up completed diaries every Friday.

Simulation

There is an increasing effort in the area of environmental studies to develop graphic displays that will simulate unfamiliar physical environments to identify preferences of potential users. These simulations are used with a survey to get citizens' responses and ratings. Graphic displays include video tape,[30] photographs,[31] games,[32] and three-dimensional models.[33]

Photographs can be used to display proposed variations of a physical setting[34] or alterations to an existing environment.[35] If time and staff are at a premium, then photographs are more feasible than video tapes. Only limited work has been done by local governments with video, but video seems

30. Donald Appleyard, et. al., The Berkeley Environmental Simulation Laboratory.

31. Kenneth Craik, "Psychological Factors in Landscape Appraisal," Environment and Behavior, vol. 4, no. 3 (September 1972); George Peterson, "A Model of Preference: Quantitative Analysis of the Perception of the Visual Appearance of Residential Neighborhoods," Journal of Regional Science, vol. 7, no. 1 (1967), pp. 19-31; Elwood Shafer, Jr. and James Meitz, "It Seems Possible to Quantify Scenic Beauty in Photographs," USDA Forest Research Paper NE-162. Upper Darby, Pennsylvania: Northeastern Forest Experiment Station, 1970. Gary Winkel, "Community Response to the Design Features of Roads," Highway Research Record, Washington, D.C. #305 (1970).

32. Robert L. Wilson, "Livability of the City; Attitudes and Urban Development"

33. Baltimore, Maryland, Neighborhood Design Study.

34. Peterson, "Model of Preference."

35. Winkel, Community Response to Roads.

to require staff expertise and funding capacity rarely available to the governments. Video also requires a more specialized setting for review by respondents, whereas photographs can be easily transported to the field to obtain respondents' preferences.

Three-dimensional models were used in the Baltimore study[35] to gather information on how children used and perceived their neighborhood environment. Such models have also been used to study user preferences for interior design characteristics, and by planners who want to convey the appearance of a proposed structure or land use plan.[36]

Gaming approaches have been used increasingly by planners. When well designed, they enable the respondent to "change" characteristics of the environment in order to estimate the relative costs and benefits of the change, and to make the necessary trade-offs to achieve the desired amenities at the least cost.[37] Exhibit 9 shows the game board used in Wilson's game.[38] Part A of exhibit 9 shows how respondents can estimate the relative importance of various utilities and services in their neighborhoods. Part B shows how the game can be used to evaluate neighborhood characteristics related to density of development, as well as the distances to various destinations. The original game board included photographs of differing densities to convey the idea of relative densities. Additional work with gaming has also yielded detailed data on citizen activities in metropolitan areas.[39]

One of the major advantages of simulation is the evaluative information it can yield. The researcher can garner data on the preferences of the respondent for one type of environment over another, or the desire to trade off

35. Baltimore, Maryland, Neighborhood Design Study.
36. See National Bureau of Standards, User Requirements in the Home.
37. Robinson, et. al., "Trade Off Games," Michelson, Behavioral Research Methods.
38. Wilson, "Livability of the City."
39. F. S. Chapin, "The Use of Time Budgets in the Study of Urban Living Patterns," Research Previews, 1966; F. S. Chapin et. al., "Human Activity Systems in the Metropolitan United States," Environment and Behavior, vol. 1 (1969).

EXHIBIT 9

Part A

WILSON'S GAME: TO ESTIMATE NEIGHBORHOOD SERVICE AND DENSITY PREFERENCES

FIREMEN
PUBLIC FIRE DEPARTMENT
WITHIN 3 MINUTES
PAID FIREMEN ON DUTY 24 HOURS PER DAY
1    $100
VOLUNTEER FIRE DEPT.
WITHIN 10 OR 15 MINUTES
UNPAID FIREMEN WHO COME FROM THEIR HOMES, WHEN THE SIREN SOUNDS
2    $50

POLICE
POLICE WITHIN 3 MINUTES
TRAINED POLICE ON DUTY 24 HOURS PER DAY - CRUISING IN PATROL CARS IN YOUR NEIGHBORHOOD
3    $100
COUNTY SHERIFF
AVAILABLE ON CALL WITHIN 30 MINUTES
BUT NOT CRUISING IN YOUR NEIGHBORHOOD
4   FREE

GAS
GAS FROM UNDERGROUND PIPES
SERVICE ENTIRE CITY FROM A CENTRAL SOURCE - BOTH HEATING AND COOKING
5    $250
GAS FROM TANKS BROUGHT BY TRUCKS
BUTANE, PROPANE, ETC.
6    $200

ELECTRICITY*
WIRES UNDERGROUND
NO OVERHEAD WIRES ON POLES IN NEIGHBORHOOD
7    $450
WIRES ON POLES OVERHEAD
8    $350

WATER*
PUBLIC WATER SUPPLY
UNDERGROUND PIPES CONNECTED TO PUBLIC RESERVOIR OR TANK, TREATED AGAINST GERMS
9    $350
WELL OR CISTERN
YOUR OWN WATER SOURCE LOCATED ON YOUR OWN PROPERTY
10    $300

TELEPHONE
TELEPHONE PRIVATE LINE
NO OTHER FAMILY CAN "LISTEN IN" TO YOUR CALL. YOU ALWAYS HAVE ACCESS TO THE PHONE
11    $250
TELEPHONE 4-PARTY LINE
THREE OTHER FAMILIES SHARE YOUR LINE - THEY CAN "LISTEN IN" TO YOUR CALL. YOU CANNOT USE THE PHONE IF THEY ARE USING IT
12    $150

SIDEWALKS
CONCRETE SIDEWALKS
ALONG THE STREETS IN YOUR NEIGHBORHOOD SMOOTH WELL DRAINED PLACE TO WALK
13    $150
GRAVEL SIDEWALKS
ALONG THE STREET IN YOUR NEIGHBORHOOD A PLACE TO WALK, OFF THE STREET
14    $50
CONCRETE CURB & GUTTER
WITH UNDERGROUND DRAINS FOR RAINWATER
15    $250
OPEN DITCHES ALONG STREETS
TO CARRY AWAY RAINWATER
16    $50

STREETS*
PAVED STREETS
IN YOUR NEIGHBORHOOD CONCRETE OR "BLACKTOP"
17    $400
GRAVEL STREETS
IN YOUR NEIGHBORHOOD
18    $300
DIRT STREETS
IN YOUR NEIGHBORHOOD
19    $50
PARKING SPACE ON THE STREET BESIDE YOUR HOUSE
STREETS MADE WIDE ENOUGH TO PARK CARS WITHOUT BLOCKING TRAFFIC
20    $200

YARDS
EXTRA BIG FRONT YD.
WITH HOUSE SET BACK AT LEAST THREE TIMES THE WIDTH OF THE STREET
21    $200
EXTRA BIG SIDE YARDS
ON BOTH SIDES OF THE HOUSE
22    $250
EXTRA BIG BACK YARD
23    $200
PARKING SPACE ON YOUR LOT
DRIVEWAY INTO YARD WITH PAVED PARKING SPACE FOR AT LEAST TWO CARS
24    $150

TREES
BIG SHADE TREES IN YOUR YARD
ALMOST FULL GROWN TREES - THE SIZE WHICH WOULD PROBABLY BE ON THE LOT BEFORE THE HOUSE IS BUILT
25    $150
TREES ALONG STREET
IN FRONT OF EVERY HOUSE
26    $100
TREES ALONG STREET
ONE OR TWO IN EACH BLOCK
27    $50
STREET LIGHTS
ON ALL STREETS AND SIDEWALKS IN YOUR NEIGHBORHOOD
28    $50

BATHROOM WASTES*
PUBLIC SEWER SYSTEM
UNDERGROUND PIPES FROM YOUR HOUSE TO A PUBLIC SEWAGE TREATMENT PLANT
29    $200
SEPTIC TANK
LOCATED UNDERGROUND ON YOUR PROPERTY - WATER DRAINS INTO SOIL SOMEWHERE UNDER YOUR PROPERTY
30    $150
OUTDOOR PRIVY
31    $50

GARBAGE & TRASH
HOME GARBAGE GRINDER
DISPOSAL FITS UNDER KITCHEN SINK-GRINDS GARBAGE - WASHES IT DOWN DRAIN - CANS & BOTTLES PICKED UP WEEKLY BY TRUCK
32    $150
GARBAGE & TRASH
COLLECTED FROM BACK PORCH TWICE EACH WEEK MEN PICK UP CONTAINERS FROM WHEREVER YOU KEEP THEM
33    $100
GARBAGE & TRASH
COLLECTED FROM STREET IN FRONT OF HOUSE TWICE EACH WEEK YOU SET CONTAINERS OUT AT SIDE OF ROAD
34    $50

RULES
1. EACH COUNTER IS WORTH $50
2. YOU MUST BUY ONE ITEM FROM EACH OF THE ✱ BOXES (ELECTRICITY, STREETS, WATER, AND WASTES)

Part B

HOW MUCH BUILDING SHOULD THERE BE ON YOUR BLOCK?

TYPICAL BLOCK - 200' x 600'

No 1
110 FAMILIES PER BLOCK
A LOT ABOUT 25' x 28' FOR EACH FAMILY   6

No 2
40 FAMILIES PER BLOCK
A LOT ABOUT 55' x 60' FOR EACH FAMILY   12

No 3
20 FAMILIES PER BLOCK
A LOT ABOUT 60' x 100' FOR EACH FAMILY   18

No 4
10 FAMILIES PER BLOCK
A LOT ABOUT 80' x 150' FOR EACH FAMILY   24

No 5
2 FAMILIES PER BLOCK
A LOT ABOUT 200' x 300' FOR EACH BLOCK   30

NEIGHBORHOOD THINGS -- HOW CLOSE TO YOUR HOUSE?

SCHOOLS

	ELEMENTARY SCHOOL GRADES 1 THRU 6	JUNIOR HIGH SCHOOL GRADES 7-8-9	A BUILDING FOR RELIGIOUS SERVICES OF YOUR FAITH
A	3 MINUTE WALK 5	3 MINUTE WALK 5	3 MINUTE WALK 5
B	10 MINUTE WALK 4	10 MINUTE WALK 4	10 MINUTE WALK 4
C	20 MINUTE WALK OR 3 MINUTE DRIVE 3	20 MINUTE WALK OR 3 MINUTE DRIVE 3	20 MINUTE WALK OR 3 MINUTE DRIVE 3
D	10 MINUTE DRIVE 2	10 MINUTE DRIVE 2	10 MINUTE DRIVE 2
E	25 MINUTE DRIVE 1	25 MINUTE DRIVE 1	25 MINUTE DRIVE 1

SHOPPING

	GROCERY STORE	DRUG STORE	BUS STOP TO BOARD BUSSES GOING DOWNTOWN
A	3 MINUTE WALK 5	3 MINUTE WALK 5	3 MINUTE WALK 5
B	10 MINUTE WALK 4	10 MINUTE WALK 4	10 MINUTE WALK 4
C	20 MINUTE WALK OR 3 MINUTE DRIVE 3	20 MINUTE WALK OR 3 MINUTE DRIVE 3	20 MINUTE WALK OR 3 MINUTE DRIVE 3
D	10 MINUTE DRIVE 2	10 MINUTE DRIVE 2	10 MINUTE DRIVE 2
E	25 MINUTE DRIVE 1	25 MINUTE DRIVE 1	25 MINUTE DRIVE 1

RECREATION

	MOVIE THEATER	PLAYGROUND WITH EQUIPMENT SUCH AS SWINGS, SLIDES, TEETER-BOARDS, ETC.	LARGE PLAYFIELD WITH BASEBALL DIAMOND, FOOTBALL FIELD, TENNIS COURT, ETC.
A	3 MINUTE WALK 5	3 MINUTE WALK 5	3 MINUTE WALK 5
B	10 MINUTE WALK 4	10 MINUTE WALK 4	10 MINUTE WALK 4
C	20 MINUTE WALK OR 3 MINUTE DRIVE 3	20 MINUTE WALK OR 3 MINUTE DRIVE 3	20 MINUTE WALK OR 3 MINUTE DRIVE 3
D	10 MINUTE DRIVE 2	10 MINUTE DRIVE 2	10 MINUTE DRIVE 2
E	25 MINUTE DRIVE 1	25 MINUTE DRIVE 1	25 MINUTE DRIVE 1

	NURSERY SCHOOL FOR CHILDREN ABOUT 2-4 YRS. OLD	PUBLIC LIBRARY BOOKS FOR LOAN, REFERENCE	PUBLIC MEETING PLACE FOR ORGANIZATIONS "A COMMUNITY CENTER" FOR YOUR NEIGHBORHOOD
A	3 MINUTE WALK 5	3 MINUTE WALK 5	3 MINUTE WALK 5
B	10 MINUTE WALK 4	10 MINUTE WALK 4	10 MINUTE WALK 4
C	20 MINUTE WALK OR 3 MINUTE DRIVE 3	20 MINUTE WALK OR 3 MINUTE DRIVE 3	20 MINUTE WALK OR 3 MINUTE DRIVE 3
D	10 MINUTE DRIVE 2	10 MINUTE DRIVE 2	10 MINUTE DRIVE 2
E	25 MINUTE DRIVE 1	25 MINUTE DRIVE 1	25 MINUTE DRIVE 1

	SHOE STORE	SHOPPING CENTER INCLUDING DRUG STORE, SHOE STORE, GROCERY STORE AND OTHERS	OUTDOOR SWIMMING POOL	SMALL PARK FOR THIS NEIGHBORHOOD ABOUT 1 BLOCK IN SIZE	SPECIAL PLAYSPACE FOR PRE-SCHOOL CHILDREN-UNDER 5 YRS
A	3 MINUTE WALK 5	3 MINUTE WALK 18	3 MINUTE WALK 5	3 MINUTE WALK 5	3 MINUTE WALK 5
B	10 MINUTE WALK 4	10 MINUTE WALK 15	10 MINUTE WALK 4	10 MINUTE WALK 4	10 MINUTE WALK 4
C	20 MINUTE WALK OR 3 MINUTE DRIVE 3	20 MINUTE WALK OR 3 MINUTE DRIVE 12	20 MINUTE WALK OR 3 MINUTE DRIVE 3	20 MINUTE WALK OR 3 MINUTE DRIVE 3	20 MINUTE WALK OR 3 MINUTE DRIVE 3
D	10 MINUTE DRIVE 2	10 MINUTE DRIVE 9	10 MINUTE DRIVE 2	10 MINUTE DRIVE 2	10 MINUTE DRIVE 2
E	25 MINUTE DRIVE 1	25 MINUTE DRIVE 6	25 MINUTE DRIVE 1	25 MINUTE DRIVE 1	25 MINUTE DRIVE 1

one amenity to secure another. Since simulations are hypothetical, however, it is difficult to be sure how the responses will correspond to actual reactions to the new development. Little longitudinal work has been done on the relative accuracy of various graphic displays.

Another problem is how to record systematically the respondents' preferences and reactions to the alternatives presented in the graphic display. A variety of attitude measurement techniques[40] can be used to obtain the degree of preference of various simulated environments.

Hypothetical Shopping Center Proposal

A ten-store community shopping center is proposed for five acres of vacant land adjacent to a middle-income, single-family, detached unit residential neighborhood. Traffic will enter and exit from existing residential streets. The project has already sparked heated controversy among neighborhood residents because of the potential disruption to "neighborhood character"-- an allowable, but vague, criterion for zoning decisions in this particular community. The staff responsible for review of the project first details the specifics of the proposed site plan, and then, using the framework developed in chapter 2, identifies the potential changes to the physical environment (see exhibit 5 for possible types of physical changes). The staff summarizes the changes to the physical environment as follows:

1. addition of ten stores, including one large supermarket, one large drug store, and convenience services (e.g., florist, barber shop, drycleaner, health food store)

2. removal of five acres of open space

3. increase of traffic volumes on nearby residential streets

---

40. Allen Edwards, Techniques of Attitude Scale Construction, New York, New York: Appleton Century Crofts Inc (1957).

4. increase of daytime and evening noise levels, due to traffic volumes

5. possible increase of pedestrian volumes on residential streets leading
    to shopping center

Choosing Impact Areas for Analysis

After looking at existing plans for the area, the staff profiles the

relevant physical conditions of the neighborhood and the socioeconomic

characteristics of residents. The findings show that there are currently no

stores in the neighborhood; that 85 percent of the households have automobiles;

and that there are no parks within a 20-block radius. From a review of five-

year-old census records, the planners find that the majority of heads of house-

holds are middle aged, and approximately 20 percent are over 65 years old.

With these data in hand, the staff reviews the list of proxy impact measures

(see exhibit 6) and checks measures likely to reflect the potential impacts

of the development. The impact areas checked include the following:

1. recreation in the informal spaces around the home: removal
    of the open space may eliminate areas used by children for play;
    changes in traffic volumes may also affect how the streets and
    sidewalks will be used; these impacts are important because of
    the lack of parks in the immediate area

2. shopping: additions of the stores may satisfy some shopping needs
    of the citizenry (although most citizens have cars and hence access
    to other stores in the community)

3. pedestrian mobility: increased traffic volumes may affect the ease
    with which people can walk around the neighborhood; the project may
    also block routes, while simultaneously adding desired destinations

4. perceived environmental quality: changes in the noise and air quality,
    generated by the traffic and construction of the development, may
    affect citizen satisfaction with their neighborhood

5. perceived personal safety and privacy: open construction sites may
    be seen as a physical threat to children in the area; increased
    traffic may affect parents' satisfaction with the safety of their
    children while playing and walking to school

Collecting Data

Given the controversy of the project, as well as possible significant degradation to the surrounding environment, the staff decides to undertake detailed analysis of the possible impacts of the project. Based on the initial choice of likely impact areas, the staff outlines the baseline data it needs, summarized in the following table, which also includes existing data sources and possible data collection methodologies they might use:

SAMPLE FORMAT FOR INITIAL REVIEW OF PROPOSED SHOPPING CENTER

Impact Area	Baseline Data Needed	Existing Data Source Data Collection Method
Recreation in informal spaces around the home	Inventory of outdoor settings used for activities	Citizen survey Direct observation
	Existing traffic volumes at selected times and points	Traffic counts
	Usage patterns, in terms of of: which activities occur in which setting who uses the setting frequency of use	Direct observation and/or citizen survey
	Perception of the setting in terms of: satisfaction with the opportunities factors contributing to dissatisfaction	Citizen survey
Shopping	Inventory of existing stores by: type location	Driving/walking survey
	Use patterns in terms of: who uses the stores frequency of use	Citizen survey and/or direct observation of area stores
	Satisfaction with shopping opportunities: factors contributing to dissatisfaction	Citizen survey

Impact Area	Baseline Data Needed	Existing Data Source Data Collection Method
Pedestrian mobility	Street layout	City engineer or walking survey
	Sidewalk location	
	Traffic volumes (see recreation)	Traffic counts
	Numbers of households re-lying upon walking to: desired destination	Citizen survey
Perceived environ-mental quality	Selected measure of noise level	Noise meters
	Perception of noise in terms of: satisfaction factors contributing to dissatisfaction	Citizen survey
Perceived personal safety and privacy	Traffic volumes (see recreation)	Traffic counts
	Perceptions of security from traffic Perceptions of security walk-ing at night	Citizen survey

Since it is summer, the staff assumes that it is the peak season for outdoor activities and decides to use direct observation and a citizen survey to collect data on recreation patterns in the informal spaces around the home.

Use of Direct Observation. The direct observation method is developed in two stages. The first involves formulation of the observation format. The staff assumes that the impacted areas will be the five-acre field where the shopping center will be built and the streets and sidewalks receiving increased traffic because of the shopping center. The first stage also assumes that it is important to record all types of activities in the open area. The planners are not concerned with what types of activities occur, such as baseball instead of kickball, but want to learn the level and general type of activity. The latter is important in order to identify alternative settings that could absorb the types of activities displaced. The format is developed with this in mind. A sample prototype is shown in exhibit 13, chapter 4.

The second stage involves the actual observations. Before going into the field, the staff decides when the observations should occur and who should conduct them. The time-frame is restricted to a 10-day period. The staff, therefore, decides to observe on Monday, Tuesday, Friday, Saturday, and Sunday of one week. They decide to have someone collect the data every three hours, at 9 a.m., noon, 3 p.m., 6 p.m., and 9 p.m., since those times could include the greatest amount of activity and coincide with the opening, closing, and rush hour traffic generated by the shopping center. The observers on the streets are to start at the beginning of a given block and walk down five or six blocks, recording any activity that occurs on either side of or directly in front of them, but not behind them. This will alleviate double counting of activities as well as ensure a representative selection of activities. Such a walking survey will take an average of 15 minutes to complete every three hours. The observer at the five-acre field is to ride a bicycle around it and record activities. Although the lot has overgrown grass, the observer will still have a clear view of activities. If it should rain at the data collection time, the observer is to go out one hour later.

Because of its limited size and the existence of a strong citizen group, the staff decides to use neighborhood residents to collect the data. They pay the residents an hourly wage for the actual amount of time used for data collection, plus the inconvenience of being there at the five collection times. The planners prefer to have the same observer for the same block for each day of observation. The citizen group chooses the observers and the staff trains them in the use of the direct observation format. They are to use a new format sheet for each data collection time. A planner goes out and makes an independent observation in at least one time period, as a rough reliability check.

When the data are collected, the staff analyzes them as discussed in chapter 4. The staff looks at where the activities occur, who participates in them, and with what frequency.

The findings indicate that the field is rarely used for group activities, perhaps because of the overgrown grass and scattered debris, although a lone jogger is often seen running around it. The streets are widely used for group activities, such as modified baseball, biking, and roller skating, and the sidewalks are heavily used by young children engaged in single or group games. They are also a focal point for couples or groups to stand or to sit in the yard and socialize. Many people, primarily the elderly, seem to use the street as a path into the area.

Use of Survey. The staff decides to develop and administer the survey itself. The staff gathers information on citizen satisfaction with settings for recreation in the informal spaces around the home, shopping opportunities, noise and security and with citizen uses of existing stores. Furthermore, they determine the number of households relying on walking to reach desired destinations. Staff members develop a questionnaire based upon relevant questions from the sample survey in the appendix. Questions on household characteristics are also included to shed light on the type of people living in the neighborhood. (If the staff had so desired, this information could also have been estimated based on census data.)

The staff pretests the survey on a sample of five to ten households. This helps ensure that the questions are understandable, accurate, and comprehensive enough to meet the needs of the study. The planners define the potential area to be impacted by the development as all streets bordering on the periphery of the five acres, going back two blocks. This area falls within the boundary of one neighborhood.

There is a total of 500 homes within the area. The planners prefer to obtain a sample of 200. They decide to do an in-person survey, and make a moderate estimate (based on the use of 20 interviewers) that the cost will run about $25 for each 20-minute interview.[41] This includes all costs: overall planning; development of survey instrument; pretesting; training interviewers; and coding, analyzing, and reporting the data. This is too expensive, so they settle for a sample of 30 to cut down on the cost of conducting and tabulating the interviews, although they recognize that their estimates will be less precise. They select their sample of 30 by assigning a number from 1 to 500 to each of the 500 homes and then using the table of random numbers (available in a statistics book) to identify which 30 households should be surveyed. Since the sample is small, a letter is sent to each household explaining the survey and setting up a time for the interview. They decide on appropriate procedures for call-backs to the households not at home.

The survey results are tabulated and analyzed by the planning department staff. Their findings are summarized as follows:

SUMMARY OF SURVEY DATA

Impact Area	Tabulated Surveys	Analysis
Recreation in informal spaces around the home	50 percent of all surveyed households very dissatisfied with current opportunities for children's play areas. Inventory shows that there are no parks in the area	Increase of traffic and potential removal of streets and sidewalks for activities will increase dissatisfaction

41. This estimate is based on figures from Weiss and Hatry, Introduction to Sample Surveys, p. 41.

Recreation (cont'd)		Planning Purpose: perhaps Dept. of Parks and Recreation should consider a neighborhood park for the area.
Shopping	Inventory: no grocery stores in the area, hence no use. Perceptions: The elderly, comprising 10 percent of those surveyed, generally did not have cars and would very much like to see a nearby grocery store	The shopping center will provide one, as well as a large drug store The shopping center will satisfy the needs of the elderly
	40 percent of the other surveyed households would prefer not to have a shopping center, although they would like walking access to a grocery store	The grocery store will be a plus, but it appears that the shopping center as a whole will still not be accepted
Pedestrian mobility	Use patterns: 75 percent of all surveyed households have grade-school children who walk to school. It appears that half of these will have to cross streets that will have increased traffic	Traffic will be increased on streets A, B, and D. Unless traffic is rerouted or new traffic lights or pedestrian tunnels are built, many of these children will be walking in an area of increased traffic hazards
	Perceptions: 100 percent of those surveyed are satisfied or very satisfied with the walking conditions in their neighborhood	The extent to which increases in traffic and noise on selected streets will affect citizens' overall satisfaction with the walking conditions is not clear
Perceived Environmental Quality	Perceptions: 25 percent of the households surveyed, especially those on street D, are dissatisfied with noise levels	Street D will be used as an exit route. We can assume that those dissatisfied will continue to be so, because of the increase in noise generated by cars. There is a possibility that the other residents may also move from somewhat satisfied to somewhat dissatisfied[1] (especially during construction of the shopping center)

---

1. Depending on the current measured noise levels and how much the change in noise will be, it may be fairer to spread the noise out by having cars use a number of streets to enter and exit.

Perceived personal safety and privacy	Perceptions: The citizens on streets A and B are currently dissatisfied with the safety of play areas for their children because of traffic	Streets A, B, and D will incur the greatest increase in traffic volumes. We can anticipate growing dissatisfaction unless corrective measures are taken on these streets.
	The majority of other surveyed households are satisfied with their security from traffic. It is doubted that these people will be affected	
	50 percent of all surveyed households are afraid to walk alone at night	It is totally unclear how the development will affect people. Crime rates are comparatively low for this particular area, and perceptions are very likely related to communitywide crime statistics

The summary survey findings can be supported with more complete tables detailing the range of responses to the various questions, as well as an inventory of existing and expected shopping opportunities, noise levels, and traffic volumes.

The staff will submit the information from the survey and direct observation to the local planning commission, together with more detailed recommendations for the project. Many of the findings could be effectively presented in a map form. For example, symbols could designate where children play, or streets could be color coded to represent changes in traffic volumes.

If time permits, the staff might also present the data from the study to a citizens' group prior to the public hearing, to obtain feedback on the utility of this type of impact analysis, and the comprehensiveness of the data presented in the study.

It becomes apparent through the collection of all of these data for a single project review that the planning department may be served best by conducting surveys and direct observations for general planning purposes as well.

The department could gain information on the perceived needs of the citizens for services, environmental amenities, open space, and other conditions. They could then detail development criteria for the area. These criteria could help preserve existing neighborhood character and enhance the future of the area for its residents. In any case, decisions based on the potential social impact of the proposed project will not be easy to make; they seldom are.

4. ESTIMATING SPECIFIC TYPES OF SOCIAL IMPACTS

The conceptual framework and methodologies described in the previous chapters are applied in this chapter to measures and data collection procedures for the seven impact areas: recreational patterns at public facilities; recreational use of informal outdoor spaces; shopping opportunities; pedestrian dependency and mobility; perceived quality of the natural environment; personal safety and privacy; and aesthetic and cultural values. Each impact area will be discussed within the framework for analysis outlined in chapter 2:

1. profile current physical and social conditions: Collect data on the current physical environment and citizen usages and perceptions. Data are needed to establish a baseline from which impacts can be estimated. (Appropriate data collection procedures are identified at this stage).

2. identify physical changes: Identify and measure potential changes to the physical environment that might impact neighborhood uses and perceptions

3. estimate impacts: Use the baseline data gathered earlier to assess how changes to the physical environment can potentially affect uses and perceptions. Estimate differences between the "with project" and "without project" profiles

4. identify alternatives to mitigate negative impacts: It may be possible to offset potential negative impacts through changes to the proposed development or to other features of the physical environment. These changes should be considered in evaluating net impacts of the development

Each of the following sections deals with one of the seven impact areas. Each section identifies a variety of approaches for estimating impacts, none of which should be used without consideration of alternatives.

Each section includes a sample summary format for displaying data on anticipated impacts. The data shown are only examples and do not relate to any one project. Not all impact areas are relevant to evaluating every proposed project.

Recreation Patterns at Public Facilities

Proposed land developments can affect the accessibility, crowdedness, diversity, and pleasantness of public recreation services by adding or removing facilities; increasing the number of potential users; or changing conditions of the surrounding environment, such as air quality or traffic volumes. All of these potential changes can affect citizens' use of the facilities and, in turn, their satisfaction with recreation opportunities.

Although we cannot predict how use patterns will change if a new development is built, we can infer, based on current perceptions and uses, how the potential changes may affect citizen satisfaction. For example, residents of a neighborhood are very dissatisfied with the lack of outdoor recreation facilities, such as swimming pools and tennis courts; and they learn that a new development will add some of these services. Planners might infer that the citizens are likely to become more satisfied with recreational opportunity once the development is built if the facilities it provides are desirable, publicly available, and can absorb demand from other overcrowded facilities. Planners must know how the residents use and feel toward the current facilities before they can make these inferences.

Planners may develop baseline data that have uses well beyond the impact evaluation of a single proposed project. For example, information on use patterns might show that the majority of elderly citizens and young children frequent the neighborhood park at least daily, whereas few children are allowed to play at the area around the basketball court because of broken glass and debris. This information might not be very useful in a decision on a specific project proposal, but it could be valuable for other planning efforts, such as programs to promote neighborhood cleanliness or to facilitate accessibility for pedestrians.

Profile Current Physical and Social Conditions

The variables listed in exhibit 10 can be used to profile the current

supply and type of public recreation opportunities and citizens' patterns and

perceptions of these facilities. The focus should be on the supply and location

of public rather than private facilities, because local government, through

coordinated line agency activity, can exercise some control over the supply

and distribution, as well as the security and cleanliness of public recreational

facilities. Hence, it can potentially mitigate or alleviate adverse impacts

to existing use patterns or perceptions of public facilities. It does not have

this jurisdictional control over the supply and accessibility of private

facilities.

Information on the supply, type, and location of existing public recrea-

tional facilities is generally available from local planning or recreation

departments. The data can be graphically displayed on a base map to help

show the location of recreational facilities relative to other neighborhood

areas. They can also be inventoried in tabular form.

Information on citizen uses and perceptions of public recreational

facilities, for both users and nonusers, can be obtained through a survey of

households in the neighborhood. Detailed information, on users only, can be

obtained through on-site surveys at local facilities.

Exhibit 11 presents a sample format for summarizing the baseline data

on recreation uses and perceptions, as well as projection data needed for

estimating impacts.

Identify Physical Changes

The following factors may prove useful in identifying possible changes

to the physical environment from the proposed development that might affect

perceptions and uses of recreation facilities:

EXHIBIT 10

SAMPLE BASELINE DATA NEEDS FOR ESTIMATING IMPACTS
ON USES AND PERCEPTIONS OF PUBLIC RECREATIONAL FACILITIES

(Columns 1 and 2 are not on a one-to-one correspondence)

Current Physical Environment	Current Uses and Perceptions	Question on Sample Survey[1]
Amount and location of parkland	Facilities used by neighborhood households (percentage of households using facility k)	17
Type and location of recreational facilities in neighborhood	Frequency of use for each facility (e.g., percentage using facility k, x or more times monthly)	18
Traffic volumes on streets used as routes to recreational facilities or surrounding the facilities	Types of users (e.g., percentage of households by age, income) using facility x times per week	16, 58
	Perceived satisfaction with public recreational opportunities	20
	Additional types of facilities desired (percentage of households citing each)	22
	Factors affecting nonuse of facilities (percentage of nonusers citing each factor)	21

---

1. Question numbers are from the sample survey in the appendix. Similar questions, tested as part of recreation effectiveness surveys, are found in Donald Fisk, How Effective Are Your Community Recreation Services?

EXHIBIT 11

SAMPLE DATA PRESENTATION FORMAT [1]

SUMMARY OF POTENTIAL IMPACTS ON USES AND PERCEPTIONS OF NEIGHBORHOOD PUBLIC RECREATION FACILITIES AS A RESULT OF PROPOSED NEIGHBORHOOD PARK WITH SWIMMING POOL

(200 households surveyed)

BASELINE DATA [2]

Current Physical Conditions (Recreation Facilities within 15 Minutes Walk or Drive)		Current Use Patterns		Current Perceptions of Recreation Opportunities		
Type	Location	Average number or percentage of households using facility 4 times a week during peak season	Types of users (clientele groups)	Households satisfied (%)	Factors affecting dissatisfaction	Desired types of recreation facilities
None	*None*	*Not applicable (N/A) since no facilities*	*N/A*	*4*	*Lack of recreational opportunities*	*Playground equipment* *Swimming Pool* *Basketball* *Park--just to sit in*

PROJECTION DATA [3]

Estimated Physical Changes			Estimated Impacts		Possible Mitigation Efforts
	Likelihood of occurrence without project	Change in number of households within 15 minutes of recreation facilities	Change in other physical conditions affecting households' satisfaction and number of households potentially affected	Change in number or percentage of households using facility by type of facility and frequency of use	
With proposed project					
Addition of Playground	*Unlikely*	*+200*	*Increased recreation opportunities will potentially increase citizens' satisfaction with available recreation opportunities*	*Unknown*	*None needed, since there are no negative impacts*

[1] Sample data are in italics.
[2] Baseline data detail current recreation opportunities and related uses and perceptions.
[3] Projection data reflect anticipated changes to baseline data, i.e., changes in recreation opportunities and ensuing impacts on uses and perceptions.

1. amount, location, and type of parkland removed or added

2. type and location of recreational facilities or programs removed or added

3. change in traffic volumes on streets used as routes to recreational facility

4. location and type of outdoor recreation areas that will be put into shadow

5. change in other physical characteristics identified as sources of dissatisfaction or satisfaction with recreation opportunities, for example, debris around a pool

Site plan specifications can provide information on the likelihood of the changes, except for changes in traffic volumes. Traffic counts and anticipated changes in volume are usually available from efforts to estimate impacts on public services. The analysis should also assess whether such physical changes are likely to occur, either in the short or long run, without the development. The data can be displayed as shown in exhibit 11.

Estimate Impacts

The effects of changes to the physical environment would preferably be described by the measure, "change in number or percentage of households satisfied with recreation opportunities at public facilities." However, since we do not know all the factors that contribute to citizens' satisfaction, nor how much each known factor contributes, we have to use proxy measures of change in some factors contributing to satisfaction:

1. number or percentage of households with access within x minutes or miles from recreation facility (by mode of travel)

2. other physical conditions likely to affect households' satisfaction with recreation opportunities at public facilities, and number of households potentially affected

Another proxy measure is the extent to which citizens change their use of recreation facilities, although it is difficult to predict reliably such behavioral changes. If data are collected before and after several types of development are constructed, an understanding of the effects of a given type of project on use patterns might result. Predicting recreation use is not generally feasible today.

Accessibility. Contour lines of equal distance can be drawn on a map around existing and proposed facilities to identify areas that are within x minutes or miles of the facility. We cannot, however, assume that the population beyond distance x will not be served by the recreation facility until we learn more about the relations among distance traveled, use, and satisfaction. An overlay showing population distribution can help identify the number of citizens who are currently within a given distance, and the number of citizens who will be within that distance after the new development. This type of assessment yields information only on potential accessibility; it does not suggest whether the population will use the facility or find it satisfactory.

Satisfaction. In estimating potential changes in citizen satisfaction, we have to identify factors that may contribute to or detract from current levels of satisfaction. Obvious factors that may detract from satisfaction are changes in the supply and crowdedness of existing facilities. (The latter can be affected by an increased demand for services generated by residents of a new development.)

To estimate potential demand for existing services, we can identify the facilities most likely to attract demand from new residents. Many new large residential developments supply their own recreational services, and, hence, will offset demand for existing municipal facilities. The percentage of new residents likely to frequent each facility can be estimated based on the anticipated sex, age, and income distribution in the new development, compared with the rates of comparable users in the existing neighborhood. Estimates of whether the project is likely to overcrowd existing facilities can then be made, based on current operating capacities. Figures on operating capacities can usually be obtained from the recreation department.

If baseline data have been collected on citizen perceptions of the quality of the services, other factors that contribute to citizen satisfaction, such as traffic volumes and surrounding air and noise quality, can also be identified. For example, in many areas parents do not let their children walk to playgrounds or community centers because of perceived traffic hazards. Traffic volumes may be the main factor in their dissatisfaction with recreation opportunities. Such factors may be either aggravated or alleviated by a new development and should be considered when estimating how potential physical changes may affect citizen satisfaction. To estimate changes in satisfaction, we can rely on inference or comparative studies. Inference involves describing the potential changes to the physical environment, and based on current levels of satisfaction and factors contributing to dissatisfaction, estimating how satisfaction levels will change. The comparative approach involves comparing several neighborhoods in which projects similar to the one proposed have been built and then identifying, through surveys, how satisfaction levels currently vary.

In the inference approach, the data can be presented in a format similar to exhibit 12; impacts can then be estimated on a step-by-step basis.

Identify Alternatives to Mitigate Negative Impacts

Potential negative impacts on recreation uses and perceptions can be offset in various ways. Shuttle services to more distant recreation services could be substituted when nearby facilities are removed. (This may be feasible only for facilities that are seen to serve a definite social need, such as boys' clubs or swimming pools. Some feel that these services can "cool off" some neighborhoods during hot summer days.) Another alternative is building small "tot lots" in areas where larger parks once existed. Impacts should be estimated with and without such potential mitigating actions.

Recreation Use of Informal Outdoor Spaces

Public spaces around the home, such as sidewalks, streets, communal open spaces, and school lots, can provide settings for a wide array of casual day-to-day activities, such as walking, playing, repairing cars, or visiting. Certain clientele groups, because of age, desired life style, or income, conduct many of their social activities in these outdoor places in their neighborhood. Because of their constant and informal nature, however, these activities may not be valued consciously by the residents. Nevertheless, a proposed development may impact the supply, accessibility, or security of the informal settings and pose a threat to the activities. Although local governments usually are not legally required to provide informal outdoor settings, they are responsible for the welfare and safety of the citizenry. Thus, they have an indirect responsibility for informal spaces.

Several recent studies by local governments have investigated how people use the outdoor spaces around their homes. The studies, conducted independently of one another, investigated the differences in type and frequency of outdoor activities given certain factors, such as increasing levels of traffic volumes;[42] constructing a highrise building in a neighborhood of lowrise buildings;[43] and locating inner-block parks in the central city.[44]

The impact of changes to the physical environment is especially important when there are no readily available and easily accessibile substitutes for the disrupted settings. For example, if traffic volumes are increased and streets

42. Donald Appleyard and Mark Lintell, Environmental Quality of City Streets.
43. San Francisco Planning and Urban Renewal (SPUR) Association, "City and Neighborhood Character."
44. Sidney Brower, "Recreational Uses of Space."

are widened, will there still be places for children to play? (Use of streets for play is often illegal and a local government cannot stop a development because of impacts on streets, but there should still be consideration of where children will play.) In the case of changes to public recreational facilities, households are more likely to seek out alternative opportunities within the community and to trade off accessibility for availability. When informal settings are changed, however, people may not be willing or able to make this same trade-off. If the nearby open lot or the sidewalks where young children play after school are eliminated, does it really help that there are substitutes 15 blocks away?

Profile Current Physical and Social Conditions

City planning or recreation departments generally do not list informal spaces around a neighborhood, so original data must be collected. Exhibit 12 shows examples of physical and social variables that can be used to profile supply, use, and perception of outdoor settings. (A sample data presentation format for summarizing potential impacts is shown in exhibit 17.)

Three basic methodologies can be used to collect information on which places in the neighborhood are used for outdoor activities, the types of people who use them, and the frequency of use. These methodologies are surveys of households; diaries kept by one or more household members; and direct observation of outdoor settings by trained observers. Information on how satisfied citizens are with the opportunities for informal recreation can be obtained through surveys. Surveys can also provide information on activities not engaged in at the time of data collection. For example, children generally play outdoors most often on weekends or in the summer. Survey questions could ask about daily or seasonal variations in use, or for a summary of use over a whole year.

EXHIBIT 12

SAMPLE BASELINE DATA NEEDS FOR ESTIMATING
IMPACTS ON OUTDOOR ACTIVITIES AND PERCEPTIONS OF
INFORMAL SETTINGS AROUND THE NEIGHBORHOOD
(Columns 1 and 2 are not on a one-to-one correspondence)

Current Physical Environment	Current Uses and Perceptions	Questions on Sample Survey[1]
Identification of outdoor settings used for activities (e.g. streets, sidewalks, open spaces)	Activities taking place in specific outdoor settings	27, 31
Traffic volumes at selected times	Frequency of activities for each setting	Not on survey; use direct observation
Noise levels: average day/ night readings on selected streets	Types of users in terms of age, income, racial, ethnic groups	16, 58, 59
	Perceived satisfaction with settings available for informal outdoor activities	31, 28
Extent of street parking		29, 30, 32
Landscaping: location of greenery	Factors affecting dissatisfaction with settings available for informal activities	

1. Question numbers are from the sample survey in the appendix. The survey's primary focus is on play areas for children. See also diary and direct observation formats for more detailed data collection purposes.

Direct observation, as employed by the city of Baltimore,[45] can be used to record outdoor behaviors and later to analyze the frequency of specific activities. (See exhibit 13 for a sample data collection format.)

Exhibit 14 gives examples of two diary formats. The first was used by Baltimore in the study previously mentioned. The second was used in a Toronto study of the effects of changes in housing types and stages in a family cycle on family time budgets of daily activities.[46]

The three methods discussed are especially appropriate for recording information on outdoor activities that are either readily known by adults or that are visible. However, the neighborhood around a child's home provides some of the most important settings for the child's activities, and children may be given short shrift if only these methods are used. A few planners have conducted workshops to study how children use and understand their neighborhood. In a recent effort in Washington, D.C., a small group of children in a downtown neighborhood worked with several planners for two half-day sessions.[47] Using a large base map, the children, ages 9 to 10, were asked to locate the general areas where they lived and played, as well as specific areas they used. The children then took the planners on a walking tour of the neighborhood and discussed the activities they engaged in at these specific places. This information was compiled on a base map prepared completely by the children. The result was a booklet the children produced describing the places they used in their neighborhood (see exhibit 15 for sample pages of

---

45. Baltimore, Maryland, Neighborhood Design Study; and Brower "Recreational Uses of Space."

46. This study is briefly discussed in Michelson and Reed, "The Time Budget."

47. Conducted at an informal session of the conference, Children, Nature and the Urban Environment, sponsored by the U.S. Forestry Service. Pinchot Institute, May 1975. See: Simon Nicholson, et. al., "Our City and the Places We Play," conference proceedings (forthcoming).

EXHIBIT 13

SAMPLE FORMAT FOR DIRECT OBSERVATION

Observer: _____

Time: Start _____

Finish _____

Site ____ Week ____ Walk ____

Date _____

Is it raining? Yes ____ No ____

Place of Observation	Steps	Sidewalk	Street	Fenced Yard	Alley	Play-ground	Vacant Lot	Other, e.g., Yard Space Not Fenced
Area								
Area B								
Area C								
Area D								
Area E								
Area F								

PEOPLE

M Man
O Woman
B Teenage Boy
G Teenage Girl
C Child

ACTIVITIES

W Walking
R Running
Si Sitting
St Standing
B Playing ball
Bi Bicycle or tricycle
P Playing--no equipment
Ps Playing on equipment
Rs Roller skating
F Fighting, rough destructive play
J Working, e.g., mailmen, police, repairmen
T Talking
H Doing housework, cleaning
A Working on auto
G Gardening
O Other

Source: Baltimore, Maryland, Neighborhood Design Study.

EXHIBIT 14

TWO SAMPLE DIARY FORMATS FOR
RECORDING OUTDOOR ACTIVITIES

Part A

What did you and your family do out of doors today?	Where did you do it?	Was there anything going on outside that bothered you or pleased you?
Tuesday		
Thursday		
Saturday		
For example: go for walk, sit outside, hang around, talk with friends, beautify yard, play, do outdoor chores, fix things, games	For example: sidewalk, steps, porch, back yard, front yard, playground, front porch, street	

Source: Baltimore, Maryland, Neighborhood Design Study.

-69-

EXHIBIT 14 - Continued

Part B

Please complete this activity record for your activities during waking hours on

_____ _____ _____ _____
(day of week)   (month)   (day)   (year)

NOTE: Any time spent working at your job (or jobs) should simply be
recorded as "At work." However, please remember to include
any lunch or coffee breaks.

	ACTIVITY	STARTING TIME	FINISHING TIME	OTHERS PARTICIPATING	LOCATION	
01						(if other, specify)
02						(if other, specify)
03						(if other, specify)
04						(if other, specify)
05						(if other, specify)
06						(if other, specify)
07						(if other, specify)
08						(if other, specify)
09						(if other, specify)
10						(if other, specify)
11						(if other, specify)
12						(if other, specify)
13						(if other, specify)
14						(if other, specify)
15						(if other, specify

OTHERS PARTICIPATING: 1 Alone, 2 Family, 3 Friends, 4 Work associates, 5 Other

LOCATION: 1 At home, 2 At work, 3 Travelling, 4 Other

Source: Michelson and Reed, "The Time Budget."

EXHIBIT 15

"SCORING THE ENVIRONMENT," BY WASHINGTON, D.C. SCHOOL CHILDREN

Part A

Part B

Empty House

This is an old House were old drunks go to hang

the Creek

We can throw rocks for fish

We can throw rocks in the water

Source: Unpublished mimeo from an information session of the conference: Children, Nature and the Urban Environment, sponsored by the U.S. Forestry Service. Pinchot Institute, May 1975. See Simon Michelson,

of the booklet). This type of workshop will not generate precise or quantitative data, but it will provide qualitative insights about neighborhood use by children.

In a series of workshops in Baltimore for the inner-block park studies, planners used a gaming technique to learn how children used the outdoors for recreation activities. The planners constructed three-dimensional cardboard and felt models that simulated the major characteristics of an inner-city rowhouse block in Baltimore. Seventeen boys and girls, ages 8 to 12, were individually asked to help put together a true story describing their outdoor play activities. Through a variety of scenarios and the use of dolls, the children identified places where they played, where their friends lived, and other conditions that would convey impressions of the neighborhood to the planning department. These "doll play games" were videotaped for later analysis and were used in planning efforts with citizens of the area.[48]

Exhibit 16 shows sample tables that could be used for analyzing baseline data on the frequency and location of activities and type of participant engaged in activities in informal settings around the neighborhood. A major intent is to obtain percentages of the total number of people in a neighborhood who use specific settings for informal outdoor activities. A second intent is to obtain relative percentages of the total number of people engaged in various activities. The first is important if a specific setting may be affected, the second is valuable in deciding which settings should be provided to meet the current activity needs of citizens. Once the frequency counts and proportions (or percentages) are tabulated, data can be graphically displayed on a base map.

---

48. Baltimore, Maryland, Neighborhood Design Study.

EXHIBIT 16

TWO SAMPLE FORMATS FOR SUMMARIZING AND TABULATING DATA
ON FREQUENCY OF ACTIVITIES IN INFORMAL OUTDOOR SETTINGSS

Total neighborhood
population = 30

Numbers shown are people observed outdoors
during time period x

Part A

Frequency of Specific Activity at Designated Setting

| Activities | Number of People Observed in | | | | Total Users per Activities |
	Streets	Sidewalks	Alleys	Porches	
Playing	10	13	8	6	37
Visiting/talking	2	7	6	4	19
Home/car maintenance efforts	4	2	4	2	12
Total users on setting	16	22	18	12	68

Part B

Types of Users of Specific Settings

| Users | Number of People Observed | | | Total Users |
	Streets	Sidewalks	Alleys	
Adult men	4	6	4	14
Adult women	2	3	6	11
Children	10	13	8	31
Total users in setting	16	22	18	56

Identify Physical Changes

In order to describe changes to the physical environment that may disrupt the settings for informal outdoor activities, the following factors could be considered:

1. amount, location, and type of private open space (e.g., vacant lot) or public open space (e.g., street, sidewalk, alley) that will be removed, added, or otherwise altered

2. change in traffic volumes

3. change in number and locations of parked automobiles

4. number of existing households whose exterior spaces (yards, balconies) will be within view as a result of the creation of new sightlines

5. location and type of areas that will be put into shadow

6. change in noise levels

7. change in other conditions that are mentioned as affecting dissatisfaction with outdoor areas

A sample display for formatting these types of data is shown in exhibit 17.

Estimate Impacts

To estimate potential impacts on how residents use and perceive outdoor recreation patterns in informal spaces, the following proxy measures of change can be used:

1. availability of physical settings that x number of people currently use for activities

2. other physical conditions affecting households' satisfaction with recreation opportunities in informal spaces around home, and number of households potentially affected

Availability. In assessing changes in the availability of outdoor places, find out if the proposed development will add usable open space, such as lots, plazas, sidewalks, or if it will remove areas currently used. The perceived availability of open space can be affected by changes not only in supply, but also in traffic volumes or shadow. For example, children may use sidewalks and streets for most of their outdoor play. Although a proposed development will

EXHIBIT 17 [1]

SAMPLE DATA PRESENTATION FORMAT

SUMMARY OF POTENTIAL IMPACTS ON CONDITIONS AFFECTING
RECREATIONAL USES AND PERCEPTIONS OF INFORMAL OUTDOOR SETTINGS
AS A RESULT OF PROPOSED SHOPPING CENTER

(200 households surveyed)

BASELINE DATA [2]

Outdoor Settings Type	Location	Current Physical Conditions — Traffic and Other Relevant Conditions	Current Use Patterns — Average Number of People Using Setting During Time x*	Types of Users (Clientele Groups)	Households Satisfied with Children's Places (%)	Factors Affecting Dissatisfaction	Households Satisfied with Adult Places (%)	Factors Affecting Dissatisfaction
Streets	A, B	*Average of 8 cars during three 15-minute afternoon periods on streets A, B, E.*	*30 during weekday 35 during weekend*	*Male children and adolescents*	*87*	*Traffic*	*45*	*Lack of outdoor places for recreation*
Sidewalks and stoops	(on streets) A, B, E		*40 during weekday 60 during weekend*	*Female adults and adolescents; M/F children*		*Broken glass*		
Open Lot	Corner of Streets F & D		*28 during weekday 32 during weekend*	*Male adults and adolescents; M/F children*		*Debris*		

* Time x is chosen by the planning department. In this case it is three weekdays and one Saturday during June.

PROJECTION DATA

Setting	Estimated Physical Changes — Traffic	Others	Estimated Impacts	Possible Mitigation Effects
Removal of open lot	*80 more cars during weekend afternoons on streets A, B.* *50-80 more cars during weekdays on streets A, B.*	*Not applicable*	Change in availability of outdoor settings currently used for recreational activities Change in other physical conditions affecting satisfaction, and number of households potentially affected	
			Removal of open lot will affect about 30 people *Traffic increases may impact the security of settings for 30-35 people in streets and 40-60 people on sidewalks*	
			Traffic increases will probably increase dissatisfaction with settings for 90 children's play	*Reroute traffic* *Identify alternative settings safe from traffic*
			Development will probably not provide outdoor setting for adults--hence will not satisfy expressed needs of 45% of citizens	*Encourage the development of an outdoor plaza in shopping center*

1/ Sample data are in italics.
2/ Baseline data detail current physical conditions, use patterns, and perceptions related to informal outdoor settings.
3/ Projection data reflect anticipated changes in the physical environment and ensuing impacts on uses and perceptions.

not change the number of these places, it may increase the volume of traffic.[49]
Due to the threat of accidents, parents may no longer perceive of sidewalks
and streets as being available to their children for play.

To estimate changes in availability, the areas currently being used can
be reviewed to see if they will be eliminated or made less desirable by the
new development. If no one is currently using public outdoor areas, it is
difficult to assess whether the addition or removal of outdoor areas will
affect the perceived availability of settings for recreational activities,
unless the changes eliminate reasons residents cited for current nonuse of
the spaces. For example, in residential neighborhoods where the homes have
large backyards where children tend to spend their outdoor time, the addition
of a tot lot may make little difference in how citizens perceive of areas
available for their children to play. On the other hand, in an inner-city
neighborhood of rowhouses where children heavily use the streets and sidewalks,
a tot lot may be viewed as a definite addition of available open space.

Satisfaction. One of the most obvious ways physical changes could affect
citizen satisfaction with informal outdoor spaces is by changing the availability of usable areas. Other factors that may contribute include changes to
traffic (which may affect security), and changes to shadow and outdoor privacy
in yards and balconies (which may affect the perceived pleasantness of the area).

To help identify conditions that will affect residents' satisfaction, a
citizen survey can be used to estimate current levels of satisfaction and
specific factors affecting them. In some neighborhoods, citizens may become
very discontent with the outdoor spaces because of increasing degradation of
air quality, changes in the types and frequencies of noise, or perhaps even

---

49. For a discussion of how traffic can affect citizens' uses of outdoor
places, see Appleyard and Lintell, Environmental Quality of City Streets.

changes in the number of people who walk through their neighborhood. They may perceive these factors as inhibiting their use of the outdoors. We cannot be sure these changes in satisfaction levels will cause changes in peoples' outdoor behaviors--all we can ascertain is that people may become more or less satisfied with available opportunities for outdoor activities. Over time, these changes in feelings may affect use patterns and overall satisfaction with the neighborhood. In order to identify such relationships, however, we would have to study a specific neighborhood at different points in time. We need baseline data in order to grasp whether potential changes engendered by the development will aggravate or alleviate the conditions cited as sources of dissatisfaction. Thereafter, we can infer whether citizens will become more or less satisfied.

Identify Alternatives to Mitigate Negative Impacts

If there is no alternative to disrupting an existing activity setting, can alternative sites be identified that will support current activity patterns and provide the same or similar amenities? If a play setting is removed, can another be found that is within calling distance of parents, or that is safe from vehicular traffic?

These concerns may initially seem minor, and too detailed for consideration by planning departments, but time and again, public hearing transcripts show that these ostensibly minor points are of major interest to households in an area about to be changed by a development.

Shopping Opportunities

Most households rely heavily upon their regional or downtown community shopping centers for services. However, smaller scale commercial facilities, such as convenience grocery stores or small shopping centers are often valued in residential neighborhoods.[50] A proposed development can affect the supply, desirability, and accessibility of commercial centers by adding or removing stores or blocking routes to them. (Although the supply of private shopping facilities is not the direct concern of the public sector, the welfare of the citizens as affected by accessibility to stores is a concern.) A change in socioeconomic characteristics of residents may also affect the types of goods carried in existing stores.

For many households, neighborhood grocery stores provide a desired commodity, and in some they answer a definite need. Removal of such resources can constitute an important social cost (in the sense of a penalty or loss) and their addition can be a benefit to households with limited mobility. Alteration of commercial facilities may be perceived as a benefit, a cost, or a negligible effect, depending on how often households use the facilities, whether transportation to other stores is available, how great a need households perceive for such facilities in the neighborhood, and their desire to see further development of this type.

This section will discuss procedures for identifying the manifest demand for neighborhood shopping facilities only briefly because the procedures are very similar to those discussed in the previous section on Recreation Patterns at Public Facilities.

Profile Current Physical and Social Conditions

The first step is to identify the existing shopping opportunities by type and location within the neighborhood. These data can be gathered by a walking

---

50. For a further discussion of the desirability of neighborhood shopping opportunities, see Richard Dewey, "Peripheral Expansion of Milwaukee County," William Ladd, "Residential Location and Shopping Patterns"; Kaplan, Marshall, and Kahn, Social Characteristics of Neighborhoods as Indicators of the Effects of Highway Improvements.

or driving survey of the area, or through records kept by planning departments.
If one of the important considerations is to preserve and protect stores heavily
used by surrounding residents, it is desirable to determine if the stores draw
their customers mostly from the immediate neighborhood or from the larger
community. This can be estimated from discussions with store owners or by
surveying a sample of customers at the store. The current status of shopping
opportunities and service areas can be summarized as shown in exhibit 19. Data
on how neighborhood people presently use and perceive of the facilities can be
collected through a survey of a sample of neighborhood residents (see sample
survey in the appendix).

To estimate impacts on shopping opportunities, the baseline data in
exhibit 18 are appropriate.

The data can be interpreted in light of some of the following questions:

1. Which neighborhood facilities are used primarily by neighborhood
   residents?

2. Do such facilities serve purposes in addition to shopping (e.g.,
   opportunities to meet friends)?

3. Do some clientele groups use certain facilities much more than others?
   Do these groups have alternative means to frequent other shopping
   facilities?

4. What specific factors seem to contribute to dissatisfaction with
   neighborhood shopping opportunities? Will these problems be remedied
   or aggravated by further development in the area?

5. Are specific types of stores lacking and needed in the view of
   current residents?

Identify Physical Changes

The most obvious change to the physical environment that can affect use
and perceptions of shopping opportunities is changing the supply by adding
or removing stores. Increasing traffic hazards, creating physical barriers, and
removing or adding pedestrian routes can affect accessibility to stores.

EXHIBIT 18

SAMPLE BASELINE DATA FOR ESTIMATING IMPACTS ON SHOPPING USES AND PERCEPTIONS
(Columns 1 and 2 are not on a one-to-one correspondence)

Current Physical Environment	Current Uses and Perceptions of Neighborhood Shopping Opportunities	Questions on Sample Survey [1]
Location and type of stores	Facilities used by neighborhood households	37
Service groups: neighborhoods or communities		38
	Average frequency of household use of stores	16,55,56,53,58,59
	Characteristics of households that frequently use facilities	44
	Factors affecting dissatisfaction	40,42
	Preference for additional types of shopping opportunities	39
	Modes of transportation to stores	

1. Question numbers are from the sample survey in the appendix.

EXHIBIT 19

SAMPLE DATA PRESENTATION FORMAT[1]

SUMMARY OF POTENTIAL IMPACTS ON CONDITIONS AFFECTING
USES AND PERCEPTIONS OF NEIGHBORHOOD SHOPPING OPPORTUNITIES
AS A RESULT OF PROPOSED SHOPPING CENTER

(200 households surveyed)

BASELINE DATA [2]

Current Physical Conditions (Stores within 15 Minutes' Walk)		Current Use Patterns			Current Perceptions of Opportunities	
Type	Location	Average number or percentage of households shopping there x times a week	Types of users	Households satisfied with location of grocery stores (%)	Stores desired	Stores not desired
None		*Not applicable*	*Not applicable*	5	*Grocery* / *Drug store*	*Department store, bars, nightclubs*

PROJECTION DATA [3]

Estimated Physical Changes		Estimated Impacts			Possible Mitigation Efforts
	Likelihood of occurrence without project	Change in number of households within 15 minutes of shopping facility	Change in other physical conditions affecting satisfaction, and number of households potentially affected	Change in number or percentage of households using facility by type of facility and frequency of use	
With proposed project	*Likely, since area is zoned for commercial development*				
Additional grocery store, and assorted service stores		+200	*Unknown*	*Not applicable, since no facilities exist where use patterns may change*	*None needed, since there are no adverse impacts*
Increase in traffic					

1/ Sample data are in italics.
2/ Baseline data detail current physical conditions, perceptions, and uses of shopping opportunities.
3/ Projection data reflect anticipated changes in the current physical environment and potential impacts on shopping patterns.

Estimate Impacts

The preferred measure, "change in number or percentage of households satisfied with shopping opportunities in the neighborhood," is difficult to estimate
for proposed developments. The impacts therefore need to be reflected through
proxy measures of change:

1. number or percentage of households within x minutes of desired
   shopping facility

2. other physical conditions affecting households' current expressed
   satisfaction with neighborhood shopping opportunities, and number of
   households potentially affected

Accessibility. Once the existing and proposed locations and types of
shopping facilities have been located on a base map, population distribution
maps can be overlaid on them to identify how many people are currently within
x minutes of a facility and how many will be within x minutes given a potential
change in supply. Refer to baseline data to identify how many current users
will be affected by changes in the location of currently used shopping facilities.

Satisfaction. If the supply and diversity of neighborhood shopping opportunities change, citizen satisfaction will probably be affected. For many citizens
who travel elsewhere to shop, the addition of local grocery stores may be of
limited value, especially for those who claim that stores bring in added
traffic, noise, and debris. For citizens reliant upon pedestrian access to
stores, the addition or removal of shopping opportunities may strongly affect
not only their access, but also their satisfaction with shopping opportunities.

In identifying potential changes in satisfaction levels, a primary concern
is to assess who will bear the costs and benefits from changes in shopping
opportunities. Baseline data from citizen surveys can be used to assess
potential changes in satisfaction. For example, if a large proportion of citizens is dissatisfied with the lack of nearby grocery stores, we can assume that

the new store is likely to increase citizen satisfaction. We cannot, except at the most general level, estimate how use patterns will be affected by a proposed change in shopping opportunities.

Identify Alternatives to Mitigate Negative Impacts

The worst social impact on shopping patterns is the removal of facilities for households who have no access to other stores. Mitigation efforts could consist of running daily bus service to other stores, or encouraging the development of food co-ops. Many of these types of programs do not come under the aegis of the planning department. Department members can, however, offer suggestions to neighborhood planning groups or public interest groups, which might be able to respond to the situation.

Pedestrian Dependency and Mobility

In an era that has seen the rapid rise of the automobile, it is often forgotten that many people depend upon or prefer their feet for transportation.[51] Many changes brought about by a proposed land development affect not only the ability but also the enjoyment of those who need or want to walk in their neighborhood. Changes to the physical environment can affect walking accessibility to neighborhood facilities by adding or removing the facilities themselves, eliminating paths to destinations, or affecting the perceived pleasantness of the walking experience. In some neighborhoods, citizens are highly dependent on walking access to mass transit; creation of barriers or increases

51. The aged are often very dependent on walking for needed goods, services, and social activities. For articles addressing their needs in urban residential neighborhoods, see Gelwicks, L. E. "Home Range and the Use of Space by an Aging Population"; Niebanck, P. L. The Elderly in Older Urban Areas; and Regnier, V. A., Neighborhood Cognition of Elderly Residents.

in traffic volumes may affect this access [52] and, hence, access to the rest of the community.

Neighborhood pedestrian paths, informally carved out by the side of the road or formally drawn into the community plan, have a purpose other than just transportation. These paths give individually perceived physical environments a structure, and according to one prominent planner, "help tie the city together, and give the observer a sense of his bearings whenever he crosses them."[53] The psychological importance of paths, although not directly studied in this section, is an important qualitative consideration when reviewing pedestrian uses.

Profile Current Physical and Social Conditions

Identify existing physical features, such as traffic volume or the condition of sidewalks or streets, that facilitate or inhibit walking. Exhibit 20 lists possible data for profiling existing physical conditions that affect walking.

Data on the physical environment and existing traffic volume can be gathered by walking surveys and traffic counters (meters), respectively, and can be displayed and described on a base map. (Traffic data are also valuable for use in estimating other social impacts, such as personal safety, recreation in outdoor areas, and perceived environmental quality.)

Where people walk, how frequently they use certain pedestrian routes, and how they perceive of their environment for walking can be assessed through surveying a random sample of neighborhood households. If this survey is not available or is not detailed enough, a special survey might be made at the facility (or other destination) that is to be displaced, to determine the percentage of users who rely on pedestrian access to it. If neither type of

52. For measures related to access to mass transit, which is often dependent on walking access, see Dale Keyes, "Transportation Impacts," in Schaenman et. al., Estimating the Impacts of Land Developments on Selected Services.
53. Kevin Lynch, Image of the City.

EXHIBIT 20

SAMPLE BASELINE DATA FOR ESTIMATING IMPACTS
ON PEDESTRIAN DEPENDENCY AND MOBILITY
(Columns 1 and 2 are not on a one-to-one correspondence)

Current Physical Environment	Current Uses and Perceptions	Questions on Sample Survey[1]
Street layout: location and width of streets	Number of households relying on walking	53, 39, 19
Physical barriers to walking	Factors affecting perceived satisfaction with walking conditions	21, 24, 26, 29, 44
Existing traffic volumes on selected streets	Availability of alternative mode of transportation	53
		Not on survey
Type and location of possible walking destinations, such as schools, mass transit stops, recreation or employment facilities, stores	Routes taken to key destinations	

1. Question numbers are from the example survey in the appendix.

survey is feasible, interviews of neighborhood store owners, recreation

center managers, or school principals can be used to obtain rough estimates

of the percentage of users who reach them on foot. These data are obviously

less rigorous. It is important to identify the various clientele groups of

people who rely most on walking to the facilities, in order to identify

later those who may bear the social costs if pedestrian access be

changed.

In analyzing these baseline data, it is also important to identify which

facilities pedestrians most heavily use. The location of the facilities and

routes to them can be marked on a base map or on an overlay. Baseline data

on frequency of use and types of users can be summarized, by facility, using

tables like that in exhibit 21.

Identify Physical Changes

Site plan specifications can be used to identify potential changes to

the physical environment from the proposed development that may affect

pedestrian mobility. The following types of changes should be considered:

1. location and width of streets (new streets added, old one blocked)

2. number of streets with sidewalks

3. traffic volumes (by time of the day; by street)

4. number and location of activity centers (stores, recreation
    facilities, schools)

5. creation or removal of barriers to pedestrian access (e.g.,
    pedestrian bridges or tunnels)

Other factors, such as the quality of the air, noise level, or odors,

may also affect walking. However, unless these factors are specifically

brought up in response to survey questions, it is difficult to say whether

they will affect pedestrian mobility.

EXHIBIT 21

TABLE SUMMARIZING DATA ON PEDESTRIAN
USES OF NEIGHBORHOOD
(Sample data)

Number of households surveyed = 400
Percentage of households with someone walking to
neighborhood destinations more than x times per month = 44%

Type of Household	Percentage of Households with at Least One Member Walking To:		
	Grocery Stores	Mass Transit Stops	Swimming Pool
Elderly households	35	28	2
Carless households	90	55	25

Identify Impacts

The following preferred measures are difficult to use for evaluating proposed development, since we cannot accurately predict how satisfaction will change with a given change in the physical environment:

1. number or percentage of households satisfied with walking conditions in their neighborhood

2. number or percentage of households satisfied with walking accessibility to desired destinations

These proxy measures of change can be used instead:

1. number or percentage of households able to walk within x minutes to desired destinations, e.g., stores, recreation facility, transit shops, school, etc.

2. physical conditions affecting households' satisfaction with walking conditions, and number of households likely to be affected

Accessibility. Plot on a base map the current pedestrian access destinations that will be removed. To estimate how many citizens live within x minutes' walking distance from the facilities, draw contours of equal distance around each facility, and make an overlay of the population distribution for the area. This will not reflect how many citizens actually walk to a facility, but it will reflect how many citizens have pedestrian access. Changes in the destination can affect these people.

To compute the number of citizens within the area who actually rely upon walking access to each facility, use the proportions gathered in the baseline data on the number of citizens, by type, within each area who walk to specific destinations. This accessibility impact may be offset (though the choice is reduced) if there is another facility with the same amenities within comparable walking distance.

Satisfaction. We do not know how citizens will adapt to physical changes in walking conditions and, hence, how much their satisfaction levels will change. At the general level, we can identify factors that may contribute to satisfaction given current expressed preferences. Using baseline data that identify which factors, such as location of grocery stores, or low traffic volumes, contribute to current levels of satisfaction or dissatisfaction, we want to estimate how the levels will be changed. For example, in one neighborhood, citizen satisfaction with walking conditions might depend on the continuance of existing low traffic volumes (and hence perceived security from traffic hazards) and good conditions of sidewalks. In another, where many households do not have cars, satisfaction may depend on the location of the grocery store. Changes in traffic hazards or sidewalks in the first area or in the number of grocery stores in the second may affect citizen satisfaction. Changes in physical conditions can then be used as a surrogate for how citizen satisfaction levels may change. These projection data can be summarized in a format similar to that shown in exhibit 22.

Identify Alternatives to Mitigate Negative Impacts

If facilities heavily used by pedestrians will be removed, or paths to such facilities will be disrupted, then questions such as the following might be asked. Can traffic from the proposed development be exited onto other streets that are not as residential or that are not so heavily used for walking? Can pedestrian walkovers be built? Can streets be differently configured to slow down traffic, or can alternative destinations be identified? Impacts should be evaluated both with and without the possible mitigation efforts.

Perceived Quality of the Natural Environment

A proposed land development can change conditions of the physical environment that may affect citizens' perceptions of air quality and noise. Changing the frequency or adding new sources of noise, or creating smoke plumes can affect citizens' satisfaction with the quality of their residential environment. Techniques for forecasting physical changes in air quality, in terms of physiological irritation, visual appearance, or odor, and in noise quality, in

EXHIBIT 22

SAMPLE DATA PRESENTATION FORMAT [1]

SUMMARY OF POTENTIAL IMPACTS ON PEDESTRIAN MOBILITY
AS A RESULT OF PROPOSED HIGHRISE APARTMENT BUILDING

(200 households surveyed)

BASELINE DATA [2]

Current Physical Conditions			Use Patterns		Current Perceptions of Pedestrian Mobility		
Destination	Routes	Peak traffic volumes (if relevant)	Households walking to destination (%)	Types of walkers (clientele groups)	Satisfied (%)	Factors affecting dissatisfaction	Desired pedestrian destinations
Grocery stores, X,Y, and 14 X street	X,Y, and Z streets	Average 20 cars an hour during early and late afternoon on Y, Z, X streets	75	Elderly households without cars; young married households	85	None cited	Mass transit stops
School, X and 10th street	X street	Same	45	Households with children	85	None cited	
Park, X and 8th street	X street	Same	75	Adults; female; adolescents	85	None cited	

PROJECTION DATA [3]

Estimated Physical Changes		Estimate Impacts		Possible Mitigation Efforts
Destinations, routes, other conditions	Likelihood of occurrence without development	Change in percentage of households within 15 minutes walk of desired destination	Change in other physical conditions affecting satisfaction, and number of households potentially affected	
Removal of convenience grocery store on 14 X street	Likely	50% fewer households will be able to walk to store (due to removal)		Encourage a convenience grocery store to locate in highrise
Increase in traffic on X street	Unlikely (unless similar type of development is proposed)		Increase in traffic may affect the perceived security of walking to school, parks	Reroute traffic; build walkway safe from traffic; put patrol guards or street safety lights on X street to ensure safer crosswalks for children going to school

1/ The example data is presented in italics.

2/ Baseline data details current physical conditions, uses, patterns, and perceptions affecting walking opportunities.

3/ Projection data reflect anticipated changes in the current physical environment and the potential impacts on uses and perceptions of the neighborhood for walking purposes.

terms of volume, type, and frequency of sounds, are discussed in another report
in this series.[54]   These changes must be estimated in order to indicate possible
change in citizen satisfaction levels.

Although this section addresses only air quality and noise, perceptions
of other factors, such as wildlife, vegetation, and water quality, may be
appropriate for assessing environmental quality in some situations.

Perceptions of environmental quality are influenced by a variety of
factors: the times at which problems occur; frequency of occurrence; the context in which they occur; and the importance citizens place on the source of
the problems. For example, a nearby industrial plant may generate intermittent
noises of relatively high frequency and volume. When surveyed, nearby residents
who have no affiliation with the plant may find the noise a constant source of
aggravation, while residents whose livelihood is dependent on the plant, may
have a higher tolerance level to the noise. If, in estimating impacts of a
nearby proposed development, we find it would generate new and louder types of
noise than an existing one, we could assume that first group would grow increasingly dissatisfied. It is less clear how the second group would react.

This example implies that a representative sample of the citizenry is
surveyed, but such sampling is not common. Most communities rely on voluntary
expressions of preference regarding noise and air quality. Research, however,
has shown that the type of people who complain may not be representative of the
entire population at risk.[55]

Federal regulations for partially ensuring air and noise quality include
standards for specific source emissions, guidelines for ambient noise levels,

54.   Keyes, op. cit., Land Development and the Natural Environment.
55.   Gerald Hoinville, "Evaluating References."

and standards for ambient air levels and pollutant concentrations. These
standards generally indicate danger points to health, but may be inadequate
indicators for assessing citizens' perceived tolerance to differing air qualities
and noise levels. Local governments may want to adopt more stringent standards
to reflect community desires.

Profile Current Physical and Social Conditions

Exhibit 23 illustrates baseline data that could be used to profile current
perceptions of environmental quality. Exhibit 24 shows the environmental
quality analysis for the shopping center discussed in chapter 3. The noise
levels at varying distances from the site of the proposed development can be
measured using noise meters. These readings will reflect the volume of outdoor
noise from all sources, such as cars, industry, and, to a limited extent,
loud human voices. Readings should be taken not only at several points, but
also at several times so that variations in noise volume can be assessed. These
readings will not provide data on the types of noises or the frequency of
occurrence for specific noises. On-site listeners can provide those descriptions.

Staff or citizens can also describe existing visual characteristics of air
pollution, such as smoke plumes and odors. Such observations can be made at
selected times and points throughout the neighborhood. Many other air pollution
problems may not be easily discernible, even though they may be physiologically
harmful.

Residents in the areas surrounding the site of the proposed project should
also be surveyed, preferably as part of a multi-purpose survey (such as the
example in the appendix), to identify current satisfaction with air and noise
quality and factors contributing to dissatisfaction. The survey would not ask
whether the respondents feel that air pollution is causing physiological harm,
but rather would assess the degree of nuisance, irritation, or dissatisfaction
they feel with the current condition of the air. People may express

EXHIBIT 23

SAMPLE BASELINE DATA NEEDS FOR ESTIMATING
PERCEIVED ENVIRONMENTAL QUALITY
(Columns 1 and 2 are not on a one-to-one correspondence)

Current Physical Environment	Current Perceptions	Questions on Sample Survey[1]
Air quality[2]	Citizen satisfaction with air quality	45
smoke plumes (times of occurrence)	Factors affecting satisfaction	46
odors (type and severity)		
eye irritation		
location of major emitting sources		
Noise[2]	Citizen satisfaction with noise	47
type of noise	Factors affecting satisfaction	48
location of major emitting sources		
volume		
pitch		
frequency of occurrence		

1. Question numbers are from the sample survey in the appendix.
2. See Keyes, Land Development and the Natural Environment, for a discussion of appropriate measurement techniques.

EXHIBIT 24

SAMPLE DATA PRESENTATION FORMAT [1]

SUMMARY OF POTENTIAL IMPACTS ON PERCEIVED
ENVIRONMENTAL QUALITY AS A RESULT OF
PROPOSED SHOPPING CENTER

(200 households surveyed)

BASELINE DATA [2]		
Current Physical Conditions	Current Perceptions	
	Satisfied (%)	Factors affecting dissatisfaction
Noise *40 dBa on Streets A,B,E*	*95*	*Airplane noise and children playing*
Air Quality *Will not be affected by the development*	*89*	*No specific source cited*

PROJECTION DATA [3]		
Estimated Changes to Noise Levels	Estimated Impacts on Satisfaction Levels (No. of Households Affected)	Possible Mitigation Effects
Increased daytime shoppers' traffic will push noise to an average of 55 dBa *Delivery trucks will generate intermittent but loud noises at night*	*Anticipated changes in noise levels will possibly move many of the satisfied households toward dissatisfaction*	*This type of development will generate traffic and, hence, noise which cannot be easily mitigated*

[1] Sample data are in italics.

[2] Baseline data detail current physical conditions and perceptions of environmental quality.

[3] Projection data reflect potential changes in the physical environment and ensuing changes to the citizens' perceptions. These data should be analyzed along with estimated changes in air quality and noise levels.

dissatisfaction about overall noise and air quality or they may identify specific sources or characteristics, such as industrial noise, smoke plumes, or odors.

Identify Physical Changes

Three general types of data are needed on physical changes:

1. addition or removal of sources of noise, thereby affecting type of noise (such as industrial or vehicular); frequency of occurrence of noise (such as day or night); magnitude of noise (such as decibel levels)

2. addition or removal of noise buffers for proposed or existing sources of noise

3. addition or removal of sources of air pollution, thereby affecting type, concentration, and distribution of physically irritating pollutants; visually perceptible smoke plumes; type of odoriferous materials

These projection data can be summarized in a format similar to exhibit 24.

Estimate Impacts

The preferred measures are the changes in the number or percentage of households satisfied with air and noise quality. The following proxy measures can more easily be used to reflect anticipated changes in perceptions of environmental quality:

1. specific physical conditions affecting households' satisfaction with perceptible characteristics of air quality, e.g., smoke plumes, odors, and number of households potentially affected

2. specific physical conditions affecting households' satisfaction with characteristics of noise levels, and number of households likely to be affected[56]

Satisfaction. An obvious way citizen satisfaction may change is if the proposed development adds or removes sources of noise or air pollutants. With

---

56. These measures would be interpreted along with objective measures of expected changes in air quality and noise levels and the number of citizens affected, as detailed in Keyes, Land Development and the Natural Environment.

regard to noise, concern is with change in types of noise, times of occurrence, and volume from the new developments. For example, the delivery trucks of a proposed grocery store may increase night noise levels on several streets and be a source of dissatisfaction to residents. With regard to air quality, the focus is on identifying changes in sources that omit smoke, odors, or visually irritating pollutants. In both cases, we have to make judgmental assessments of how citizen satisfaction may change.

Judgments of noise may be based on prior calibration of noise levels with citizen satisfaction. The calibration may be based on surveys of citizens exposed to different noise levels.

Another way to infer noise impacts is through simulation. For example, the staff could tape-record different noise levels from surrounding neighborhood settings in the community, some of which would be comparable to the levels expected after development. Respondents would then rate their responses to the various noise levels on a scale ranging from "not objectionable" to "very objectionable."

Another approach for estimating perceived environmental quality is through analogies. This approach compares the area where the development is proposed with an area that has the air quality or noise levels expected to result from the development. The areas should be similar in topography, population character-istics, and land use. If such analogous situations can be found, a mini-survey in the area with the higher levels of noise or pollution can be conducted to estimate citizens' satisfaction with the environment. Comparing the results with a survey in the area under study will indicate whether the potential changes in environmental quality will affect satisfaction. A basic problem with the use of analogies is that people can adapt to a phenomenon. Due to the speed with which people adapt to change, we will not learn their initial reaction to the development unless the change in the comparison area is relatively new.

Before-and-after studies can be conducted to learn how different types of development affect citizens' perceptions of environmental quality. A random sample of citizens is surveyed before a development is built; the same or another sample is surveyed afterwards to identify the number of households with changed perceptions. These findings can later be used for comparative purposes in estimating how similar types of developments proposed for similar neighborhoods will affect perceptions. Unfortunately, however, this still would not fully clarify how people adapt to such changes over time.

Identify Alternatives to Mitigate Negative Impacts

Noise and air quality problems can be mitigated to a limited extent through project engineering. For planning purposes, the community may decide on development patterns that avoid concentrating annoying sources near certain residential areas. Decision makers may also require that all developments proposed for an area have appropriate noise barriers or engineering devices to offset potential negative effects.

If planners decide to develop noise standards (noise volumes which cannot be exceeded) based on citizen perceptions, in conjunction with existing federal standards, they might want to put together noise perception surveys for a variety of residential, residential/commercial, and industrial neighborhoods with differing noise volumes. Noise measurements could be taken at sample sites at selected times. The staff could then survey a sample of citizens in each area to assess their current levels of satisfaction. These perceptions could be analyzed vis-a-vis noise levels to identify which volumes are satisfactory for which types of citizens (defined by type of residents, or socioeconomic characteristics), and in which types of settings. It could be assumed that louder noises would be tolerated around an industrial area than around a strictly residential area. Outer limits of noise volumes could be based upon perceived tolerance levels of citizens.

Personal Safety and Privacy

How people perceive of their security can affect their activities. For example, elderly citizens perceiving a threat from automobiles may hesitate to take walks; many people are afraid to walk alone at night. The perceptions may or may not be related to the actual risks involved, and therefore they should be considered in addition to "true" hazards, such as crime rates or traffic volumes. The effect of potential increases in traffic on citizens' behavior have already been discussed. Here we will sum up how to estimate citizens' perceptions of their physical security from traffic and crime.

Peoples' ability to control their privacy in the spaces around their homes is strongly influenced by the density and design of surrounding development. The need for privacy is very much a function of the cultural and social milieu. People who have grown up in walk-ups in big cities may think nothing of sitting on the fire escape in full view of their neighbors, whereas people who have lived in rural single-family detached units may find their privacy severely impaired by a new nearby highrise apartment building. Recent research shows that many people highly value privacy in the outdoor areas of their homes.[57] In a study of homeowners in Australia about 25 percent of the households in each community rated privacy first as an important dwelling unit feature.[58]

Profile Current Physical and Social Conditions

The approach to this problem is very similar to that discussed in the section on Perceived Quality of the Natural Environment. A survey of a sample

---

57. Elizabeth J. Harman and John F. Betak, "Some Preliminary Findings on the Cognitive Meaning of External Privacy in Housing," in Man-Environment Interactions; John Lansing, Robert Marans, and Robert Zehner, Planned Residential Environments.

58. P. N. Troy, "Residents and Their Preferences: Property Prices and Residential Quality," Regional Studies, Vol. 7, pp. 183-192.

of neighborhood residents can be used to assess their current levels of satisfaction with their privacy and security, and to identify specific sources of
characteristics contributing to dissatisfaction. This information can then be
evaluated in light of objective measures of the physical environment, such as
traffic flows, location of street lights, heights of surrounding buildings, or
local crime rates. (Questions 45-48 on the survey in the appendix are examples
of questions that can be asked to identify baseline attitudes toward security.)

Identify Physical Changes

Unless respondents specify, in the baseline data, the factors that contribute to or detract from their satisfaction with security and privacy, there
is really no way to be sure which types or magnitudes of changes in the physical
environment will affect their perceptions. It is not possible to conclude
definitely that so many more cars per hour will change citizens' perceptions
of their security from traffic; that bringing in a housing development for a
different socioeconomic group will change perceptions of safety in the neighborhoods; or that the construction of highrises overlooking backyards will
change perceptions of privacy.

Based on limited studies and experiences, changes in traffic or sightlines
seem like important factors in changing perceptions of security and privacy,
but we cannot conclude that they are determining factors. Unless specific
neighborhoods are monitored over time, we will have very limited knowledge of
what physical factors most strongly affect perceptions of security and privacy
for certain socioeconomic groups.

Estimate Impacts

Once more, we must rely on proxy measures to reflect potential changes
in perceptions:

1. traffic volumes and other conditions affecting households' satis-
    faction with physical safety from traffic, and number of households
    potentially affected

2.   physical conditions affecting households' satisfaction with security from crime, and number of households potentially affected

3.   identification of features of the proposed development that may pose hazards to children, and number of children potentially affected

4.   sightlines, pedestrian volume, or other conditions that might affect households' satisfaction with privacy, and number of households potentially affected

From baseline data on both physical conditions and perceptions of privacy, we can infer which changes in physical conditions might affect perceptions. For example, to estimate possible impacts of a new highrise on privacy, we must assess, through geometric analysis of the proposed height of the developments, how many yards and balconies of existing households will be overlooked. If citizens have rated highly their satisfaction with outdoor privacy, we can qualitatively judge that they will not be satisfied with this change. In another neighborhood, if residents cite high pedestrian traffic as inhibiting their privacy, then a proposed development could be evaluated in light of its impact on the volume of pedestrian traffic.

To estimate the impacts on security from a new development, consider two factors: changes in traffic volumes, and specific design features of the development, such as a fish pond that may be attractive, but dangerous, to children.

Comparative studies are useful for estimating impacts on perceived security and privacy. Comparative studies of two similar neighborhoods, one with a specific development and one where a similar development is proposed, are useful. In estimating impacts on perceived security and privacy, citizen perception of security and privacy can be measured in the two neighborhoods. The differences in the responses in the two places can be partially attributed to the specific development under study. This information can be compared to the levels of satisfaction of the citizens in neighborhoods where the changes are proposed. If the latter are satisfied and the former are not, we can attribute some of the differences to the development and we can hypothesize that the latter will move toward dissatisfaction.

If there is much concern about impacts on security and privacy generated by a popular type of development, conduct before-and-after studies of several such developments to identify changes in the level of satisfaction and citizens' views of the factors contributing to them. This information can be used in evaluating proposals for similar developments.

Identify Alternatives to Mitigate Negative Impacts

Can traffic be exited onto nonresidential streets? Can the proposed structure be situated so that the number of new sightlines will be lessened? Such questions may be used to identify mitigation measures.

Exhibit 25 shows one way the impacts on perceptions may be summarized.

Aesthetics and Cultural Values

Man-made or natural characteristics of a neighborhood can strongly contribute to its perceived aesthetic and cultural attractiveness. A proposed development may remove or alter characteristics of the neighborhood that have historic, cultural, or aesthetic value to the residents. There are growing efforts by locally mandated design review boards,[59] historic societies, and other groups to protect, enhance, or preserve such characteristics.

Federal, state, and local legislation and litigation have increasingly used constitutional and common law to justify the consideration of aesthetics in land use decision making.[60] In some states, including New York and Oregon,

---

59. Donald C. Ashmanskus, "Design and Site Review Boards."
60. "Aesthetic Nuisance: An Emerging Cause of Action"; William Agnor, "Beauty Becomes a Comeback"; Robert Broughton, "Aesthetics and Environmental Law"; Leighton, "Aesthetics as a Legal Basis for Environmental Control"; Sidney Z. Searles, "Aesthetics in the Law"; Dennis Minano, "Aesthetic Zoning."

EXHIBIT 25

SAMPLE DATA PRESENTATION FORMAT[1]
SUMMARY OF POTENTIAL IMPACTS ON PERCEIVED
PERSONAL SECURITY AND PRIVACY AS A RESULT
OF A PROPOSED HIGHRISE APARTMENT BUILDING

(200 households surveyed)

BASELINE DATA[2]

Current Physical Conditions	Satisfied (%)	Factors Affecting Dissatisfaction
Neighborhood traffic accident rate - *2 last year on streets X, Y, Z*	*88% satisfied with security from traffic*	
Neighborhood traffic volumes *average 20 cars an hour during afternoon*		
Neighborhood crime rates *considered irrelevant to this project*	*80% afraid to walk alone at night*	
Number and location of existing building that afford clear sightlines into existing yards and balconies *none*	*80% satisfied with privacy*	*Too many people around outdoors*

PROJECTION DATA[3]

Estimated Physical Changes	Estimated Impacts	Possible Mitigation Efforts
Increase in traffic on street due to residential trips (average 3 per apartment) 3 X 150 = 450 automobile trips	**Change in traffic volumes and other conditions affecting satisfaction with physical safety from traffic, and number of households potentially affected:** *An increase of 450 daily trips, 75% potentially affected*	*No recourse from increased traffic*
Which physical changes will affect crime rates unknown	**Change in physical conditions affecting satisfaction with security from crime, and number of households potentially affected:** *Unknown*	
New highrise in neighborhood of single-family detached units	**Change in sightlines, pedestrian volume or other conditions that affect satisfaction with privacy and number of households likely to be affected:** *50% of households will have new sightlines into their yards and balconies*	*Unfeasible to consider repositioning of windows, since homes are on all sides*
Massive construction operation for one year	**Identification of features that may be harmful to children, and number of children potentially affected:** *Construction site, unless well barricaded, may be a hazard*	*Ensure surveillance around construction site*

1/ Sample data are in italics.

2/ Baseline data reflect current physical conditions and related perceptions of security (from traffic and crime) and privacy (in outdoor areas--yards, balconies).

3/ Projection data reflect changes in current physical conditions and how perceptions may be affected.

aesthetics alone can provide the basis for a land use decision; in others, the focus is not so much upon the physical attractiveness of the development itself, but how well the development will fit into the "character" of an area as interpreted according to historical,[61] cultural, or design criteria.

Profile Current Physical and Social Conditions

A citizen survey can be used to identify current physical features, such as landscaping, views, landmarks, or street cleanliness, that residents value for aesthetic and cultural significance. Citizen surveys can also be used to identify characteristics that are disliked. Sample baseline data needs are shown in exhibit 26. Several types of data collection procedures can be used to inventory objective characteristics of physical features.

Landscaping. Several approaches are available for inventorying scenic and landscape variables.[62] They often focus on large undeveloped wild areas, such as river canyons and forests, and not on the variables relevant to urban residential neighborhoods. (Current research efforts are developing methods for inventorying design and landscape variables that affect perceived urban neighborhood attractiveness.[63]) Some communities or rural areas may find these

61. Malcolm Baldwin, "Historic Preservation in the Context of Environmental Law"; "A Bibliography of Periodical Literature Relating to the Law of Historic Preservation"; Paul E. Wilson and H. James Winkler, "The Response of State Legislation to Historic Preservation."
62. For reviews of current methodologies for the inventorying and objective appraisal of aesthetic attributes of the environment, see Julius Gy. Fabos, "An Analysis of Environmental Quality Ranking Systems"; and Washington Environmental Research Center, "Aesthetics in Environmental Planning." For examples of the methods, see Luna Leopold, "Landscape Aesthetics"; Luna Leopold, "Quantitative Comparison of Some Aesthetic Factors Among Rivers"; R. Burton Litton, et. al., "An Aesthetic Overview of the Role of Water in the Landscape prepared for the National Water Commission by the Department of Landscape Architecture; and Elwood L. Shafer, Jr., John Hamilton, and Elizabeth Schmidt "Natural Landscape Preferences: A Predictive Model."
63. See George L. Peterson, "Measuring Visual Preferences of Residential Neighborhoods."

EXHIBIT 26

SAMPLE BASELINE DATA FROM ESTIMATING IMPACTS ON AESTHETICS AND CULTURAL VALUES
(Columns 1 and 2 are not on a one-to-one correspondence)

Current Physical Environment	Current Perceptions	Questions on Sample Survey[1]
Location, type, and supply of landscaping and vegetation	Identification of visually attractive buildings, places, or conditions	11, 12
Location of bodies of water	Identification of visually unattractive buildings, places, or conditions	9, 10
Location of historic districts, landmarks, or socially valued buildings or places	Percentage of households satisfied with view opportunities	13
	Percentage of households satisfied with landscaping	15
Current levels of street maintenance and cleanliness		5, 6, 7
Location of distinct architectural styles	Percentage of households satisfied with repairs and cleanliness of streets, yards, sidewalks	Not on survey
Views of noticeable importance, e.g., mountains, water, cityscape (the determination of noticeable importance is at the discretion of the policy makers)	Identification of historic, cultural, or scientific landmarks, rated in terms of their rarity and perceived importance	51, 52
	Identification of unique neighborhood places	

1. Question numbers are from the survey in the appendix.

inventory methods valuable for planning or program evaluation. These methods
locate, on some objective (or at least systematic) and quantitative basis, the
landscape resources of a geographic area. They can then be used to chart
changes in the amounts and types of vegetation from natural and man-made forces,
including those resulting from development. Such inventorying has advantages
for planning and extensive program evaluation. It has limited value for project
review, although the site under consideration can be surveyed prior to development.

Landmarks. Existing landmarks, architectural styles, or other structures
of historic or cultural significanace in the area to be impacted by the development often can be identified with the aid of historical societies or local
universities. Inventories are valuable if a city intends to preserve such
areas. Many communities have seen such landmarks threatened or destroyed by new
development. One community that took steps to prevent this destruction is
Dallas, Texas. Its Urban Design Division helped develop historic landmark desig-
nation criteria.[64] Such criteria can be based on surveys of citizens, tourists,
scholars, and other relevant groups to identify structures, sites, or areas
that hold significance for specific clientele groups. These opinions help to
establish priorities for preservation.

Views. Existing view opportunities can be identified by on-site visits or
geometric analyses of the position and heights of buildings and by a qualitative assessment of the nature of the view (e.g., mountains versus buildings).

---

64. City of Dallas, Urban Design Division "Historic Landmark Criteria,"
Dallas, Texas, City Planning Department. The federal government has also
published a report for local governments documenting possible funding sources
for historic preservation: National Trust for Historic Preservation with the
Advisory Council on Historic Preservation and Legislative Reference Section
of the Library of Congress, Guide to Federal Programs Related to Historic
Preservation.

In a recent study in San Francisco on the impact of highrise developments[65], planners collected baseline data on existing view opportunities. On base maps of neighborhoods was superimposed a template, marked off in angles to represent degree and direction of view, to identify how existing buildings have blocked views of the area. The base maps showed the elevations and heights of structures. The baseline data were used to estimate how the heights of the proposed highrises would obstruct existing views.

Street Cleanliness. Street cleanliness may be changed by the new development, although it is hard to project the extent of change. At the Urban Institute a method has been developed for rating the cleanliness of urban streets. It uses a trained observer driving through selected streets and giving "a numerical rating to the litter conditions on a street or alley. The rating is the basis of measuring differences and changes over time and among neighborhoods."[66]

Citizen Perceptions. To complement the inventorying and rating of current physical conditions, citizens can be surveyed to obtain their overall rating of neighborhood attractiveness. They can be asked to identify specific man-made or natural factors that most contribute to or detract from aesthetic attractiveness. It is not clear, however, whether people can break down the visual components of their environment and identify exactly what is most influential on their perceptions.[67] Results can be summarized as shown in exhibit 27.

Identify Physical Changes

Obvious changes to the physical environment, which can spin off secondary changes, including the following:

65. San Francisco Planning and Urban Renewal Association, "City and Neighborhood Character."
66. Louis Blair and Alfred Schwartz, How Clean is Our City?,
67. Peterson, "Measuring Visual Preferences."

EXHIBIT 27

SAMPLE DATA PRESENTATION FORMAT[1]

SUMMARY OF POTENTIAL IMPACTS ON AESTHETICS
AND CULTURAL VALUES AS A RESULT OF
PROPOSED HIGHRISE APARTMENT BUILDING

(200 households surveyed)

BASELINE DATA[2]

Current Physical Conditions	Scholars' rating of rarity	Current Perceptions		
		Percentage satisfied	Attractive factors	Unattractive factors
Neighborhood attractiveness: *Pond on X Street; large, old trees border street*	*Not applicable*	94% rate neighborhood as very attractive	*Landscaping Pond on X street Colonial architecture Views*	*Modern building at X and 10th streets Gravel quarry*
View opportunities: *Views of mountains currently available to 200 households in this neighborhood*	*Not applicable*	100%	*Mountain*	*None currently*
Landmarks: *First log cabin in community located here*	*Rare for this community*	100%	*80% cite cabin as important*	

PROJECTION DATA[3]

Estimated Physical Changes	Estimated Impacts	Possible Mitigation Efforts
Neighborhood conditions: *Remove open area around pond*	Change in attractive physical conditions of neighborhoods: *Some of the 94% will probably be dissatisfied with disruption to landscaping and views*	*Add trees, greenery*
View opportunities: *Highrise will block view of mountain*	Number of households whose view opportunities are blocked, degraded, or improved: *50% of households will have blocked views of the mountains; we assume they will be dissatisfied*	*Locate structures so that the fewest number of households will have blocked views*
Landmarks: *No effect*	Perceived importance of landmarks to be lost or made inaccessible or accessible: *No effect*	*Not needed*

1/ Sample data are in italics.

2/ Baseline data detail current physical conditions and related aesthetic preferences and cultural values.

Initial Changes	Secondary Changes
Change in heights of buildings	Number of households with loss of view opportunities
Construction of a building on undeveloped land	Amount and location of open space and greenery removed
	Changes to bodies of water
	Change in street cleanliness
Removal of existing structures	Number of cultural or historical architectural structures or sites removed or altered
Change in traffic volumes	Number and type of changes to private yards, sidewalks, and greenery to absorb changes in traffic volumes
Change in form of proposed structures as compared to existing structures	Dissimilarities of structures in terms of design characteristics: textures; colors; shapes; materials

Most changes can be identified from detailed review of the proposed site plan specifications in view of existing physical characteristics of the area.

Some changes, such as street cleanliness, cannot really be predicted by inference. An alternative approach is to identify how analogous development in similar environments has affected street cleanliness.

To estimate changes to view opportunities, superimpose a template (marked off in degrees and angles) on a base map of existing and proposed structures. Place the template at the face (or front) of existing structures, marked according to heights and elevations, and estimate how much the proposed structure will block views from existing structures.

The projected changes can be summarized as shown in exhibit 27.

Estimate Impacts

Identify which changes to the physical environment will result in the

following changes:

1. physical conditions of neighborhoods that are currently rated as physically attractive

2. number of households whose view opportunities will be blocked, degraded, or improved

3. perceived importance of landmarks to be lost or made inaccessible

Neighborhood Attractiveness. Baseline data show which characteristics of the neighborhood citizens rate highly for their attractiveness. If a proposed development removes or alters features rated as very attractive, we can assume that citizens will be dissatisfied. For example, if the proposed development will remove a valued historic church, we could infer that the citizens will be dissatisfied.

Changes, removals, or additions of different types of development or landscaping can also be simulated through graphic displays and shown to residents in order to rate their preference of the changes. To estimate responses to the simulated environmental alteration, develop the visual simulation (photographs, films, video tape, models, and sketches) of the existing environment with the proposed changes built in, and construct a structured response format on which people rate their preferences for the proposed design presented in the display.[68]

The choice of which types of graphic display to use varies according to staff time, budget, and availability of simulations already prepared by the

_____

68. These studies discuss possible simulation methodologies: Kenneth Craik, "The Comprehension of the Everyday Environment," Journal of the American Institute of Planners, vol. 34 (January 1968); Kenneth Craik, "Psychological Factors in Landscape Appraisal," Environment and Behavior, vol. 4, no. 3 (September 1972); Peterson, "Measuring Visual Preferences"; Donald Appleyard, et. al., The Berkeley Environmental Simulation Laboratory; Elwood Shafer, Jr. and James Mietz, "It Seems Possible to Quantify Scenic Beauty in Photographs"; Gary Winkel, "Community Response to the Design Features of Roads."

developer.   One study on responses to the design features of roads used photo-

retouching techniques to simulate removal of such elements as billboards and

overhead utilities.[69]

A major limitation to the use of graphic simulation for estimating user

preferences is the lack of knowledge about the reliability of the findings.

There has been too little effort on reliability testing to know the extent to

which responses to a simulation will correspond to responses to the actual

setting.

Views.   Impacts are assessed by geometrical analysis of physical changes

to view opportunities, as previously discussed. A base map can show which house-

holds will have changed view opportunities.

Landmarks.   Relevant clientele groups can be surveyed to determine the

historical, scientific, architectural, archaelogical, or cultural significance

of structures to be removed.   In assessing significance, consider the distance

to a comparable structure or site, and its perceived rarity.

Identify Alternatives to Mitigate Negative Impacts

If it appears that the design of the proposed structure, or the potential

changes to the physical environment, will adversely affect citizen satisfaction,

then design changes, such as increased landscaping (to offset removal of open

space or addition of unattractive structures) or decreased height of the pro-

posed building (to offset view obstruction), can be sought.   The possibilities

69.   Winkel, Ibid.

for design changes are many, depending upon the design and function of the proposed structure.

Overall Satisfaction

In evaluating a proposed land development, we need to learn how the changes to the physical environment resulting from the development will affect the citizens' overall satisfaction with their neighborhood. An estimate of current overall satisfaction can be made by surveying citizens as part of the collection of baseline data. This type of summing-up question on a survey allows the respondents to weigh all the pros and cons about their residential environment.

If a local government engages in a wide range of studies of the impacts of different types of development on the physical environment of the neighborhood and the resulting effects on citizens' satisfaction, then at some point it may be possible to estimate impacts on overall satisfaction.

BIBLIOGRAPHY

Case Studies

Appleyard, Donald, and Carp, Francis. The Bart Residential Impact Study: A Longitudinal Empirical Study of Environmental Impact. Working Paper #205. Bart #12. Berkeley, California: Institute of Urban and Regional Development. University of California, Berkeley, February 1973.

Appleyard, Donald, and Lintell, Mark. Environmental Quality of City Streets. Working Paper #142. Berkeley, California: Institute of Urban and Regional Development, University of California, Berkeley, December 1970.

Brower, Sidney. "Recreational Uses of Space: An Inner City Case Study." Social Ecology Man-Environment Interactions, ed. by Daniel Carson. Proceedings of the fifth annual conference of the Environmental Design Research Association. Milwaukee, Wisconsin: University of Wisconsin, Milwaukee, 1974.

Burkhardt, Jon E. "Neighborhood Social Interaction: Measurement and Predictions of Change." Mimeographed. Washington, D.C.: Federal Highway Administration, 1969.

Cooper, Clare. Residents' Attitudes Towards the Environment at St. Francis Square, San Francisco: A Summary of the Initial Findings. Working paper #126. Berkeley, California: Institute of Urban and Regional Development. University of California, Berkeley, July 1970.

Harman, Elizabeth J., and Betak, John F. "Some Preliminary Findings on the Cognitive Meaning of External Privacy in Housing." In Man-Environment Interactions, ed. by Daniel Carson. Proceedings of the fifth annual conference of the Environmental Design Research Association, Milwaukee, Wisconsin: University of Wisconsin, Milwaukee, 1974.

Kaplan, Marshall, Gans, and Kahn. Social Characteristics of Neighborhood as Indicators of Effects of Highway Improvements. Washington, D.C.: U.S. Federal Highway Administration, February 1972.

Lansing, John, Marans, Robert, and Zehner, Robert. Planned Residential Environments. Ann Arbor, Michigan: Institute for Social Research, The University of Michigan, 1970.

Lee, Terrence. "Urban Neighborhood as a Socio-Spatial Scheme." Human Relations Volume 21 (1968).

San Francisco City Planning Department. Social Reconnaissance 1970. Preliminary Report #6. San Francisco, California, 1970.

San Francisco Planning and Urban Renewal Association. "City and Neighborhood Character." In Impact of Intensive High Rise Development in San Francisco: An Evaluation of Alternate Development Growth Strategies. Step 1, Part B. A Final Feasibility Report, San Francisco, California, April 1973.

Southworth, Michael, and Southworth, Susan. "Environmental Quality in Cities and Regions: A Review of Analysis and Management of Environmental Quality in the United States." Town Planning, July 1973.

Troy, P.M. "Residents and Their Preferences: Property Prices and Residential Quality." Regional Studies, Vol. 7. (1973).

U.S. Army Corps of Engineers. Social Impact Assessment: An Analytical Bibliography. IWR #74-76. Fort Belvoir, Virginia: Institute for Water Resources, (October 1974.)

U.S. Department of Transportation. Social and Economic Effects of Highways. (Distributed by NTIS) Washington, D.C.: Department of Commerce, May 1974.

Yin, Robert. Participant Observation and the Development of Urban Neighborhood Policy. New York, New York: New York City Rand Institute #4-962, May 1974.

Zehner, Robert, and Marans, Robert. "Residential Density, Planning Objectives and Life in Planned Communities." American Institute of Planners' Journal, vol. 39, no. 5 September 1972.

DATA COLLECTION METHODOLOGIES

Appleyard, Donald, et. al. The Berkeley Environmental Simulation Laboratory: Its Use in Environmental Impact Assessment. Working Paper #206. Berkeley, California: Institute of Urban and Regional Development, University of California, February 1973.

Baltimore, Maryland. City Planning Department. Neighborhood Design Study. Progress Report #3. Baltimore, Maryland: Baltimore Community Renewal Program, August 1973.

Blalock, Hubert M. An Introduction to Social Research. Englewood Cliffs, New Jersey: Prentice Hall, Inc., 1970.

Blalock, Hubert M. Social Statistics, 2nd ed. New York, New York: McGraw-Hill Book Company, 1972.

Blalock, Hubert M. and Blalock, Ann B., eds. Methodology in Social Research. New York, New York: McGraw-Hill Book Company,1968.

Converse, P.E. "Time Budgets." In International Encyclopedia of the Social Sciences, vol. 16. New York, New York: Macmillan, 1968.

Edwards, Allen L. Techniques of Attitude Scale Construction. New York, New York: Appleton Century Crofts, Inc., 1957.

Fabos, Julius Gy. "An Analysis of Environmental Quality Ranking Systems." In Recreation Symposiums Proceedings. State University of New York, College of Forestry. Syracuse University, October 12-14, 1971.

Festinger, L. and Katz, D., eds. Research Methods in the Behavioral
    Sciences. New York: Dryden Press, 1953.

Fisk, Donald. How Effective Are Your Community Recreation Services?
    Washington, D.C.: Bureau of Outdoor Recreation, April 1973.

Hoinville, Gerald. "Evaluating Community Preferences. Summary Report of
    SCPR Development Work." Mimeographed. London. Social and Community
    Planning Research.

Leopold, Luna. "Landscape Aesthetics." Ekistics, vol. 29, no. 173 (Spring
    1970). _____. "Quantitative Comparison of Some Aesthetic
    Factors Among Rivers." U.S.G.S. Circular 620. Washington, D.C., 1969.

Marans, Robert. "Survey Research." In Behavioral Research Methods in
    Environmental Design, ed. by William Michelson. Stroudsburg,
    Pennsylvania: Dowden, Hutchinson, and Ross, Inc., 1975.

Michelson, William and Reed, Paul. "The Time Budget." In Behavioral Research
    Methods in Environmental Design. ed. by William Michelson.
    Stroudsburg, Pennsylvania: Dowden, Hutchinson and Ross, Inc., 1975.

National Bureau of Standards Report. User Requirements in the Home--Data
    Collection Methodology--A State of the Art Report. NBS Report 10 852.
    Washington, D.C.: U.S. Department of Commerce, December 1971.

Oppenheim, A. H. N. Questionnaire Design and Attitude Measurement. New York:
    Basic Books, 1966.

Osgood, Charles E., Succi, George, and Tennenbaum, Percy. The Measurement
    of Meaning. Urbana, Illinois: University of Illinois Press, 1967.

Peterson, George L. "Measuring Visual Preferences of Residential Neighbor-
    hoods." Ekistics, vol. 23, no. 136 (May 1967).

Robinson, Ira, et. al. "Trade-Off Games." In Behavioral Research Methods
    in Environmental Design, ed. by William Michelson. Stroudsburg,
    Pennsylvania: Dowden, Hutchinson, and Ross, Inc., 1975.

Scott, J.C., and Chanlett, Eliska. Planning the Research Interview.
    Chapel Hill, North Carolina: Laboratory for Population Statistics,
    University of North Carolina, 1973.

Shafer, Elwood, Jr., Hamilton, John, and Schmidt, Elizabeth. "National
    Landscape Preferences: A Predictive Model." Ekistics, vol. 29, no.
    173 (April 1970).

Shafer, Elwood, Jr., and Mietz, James. "It Seems Possible to Quantify Scenic
    Beauty in Photographs." U.S.D.A. Forest Service Research Paper NE-162.
    Upper Darby, Pennsylvania, Northeastern Forest Experiment Station,
    1970.

Stein, Martin. "Application of Attitude Surveys in Transportation Planning and Impact Studies: A Case Study of Southwest Washington, D.C." Traffic Quarterly, vol. 29 (January 1975).

Washington Environmental Research Center. Aesthetics in Environmental Planning. EPA-600/5-73-009. Washington, D.C.: U.S. Environmental Protection Agency, November 1973.

Webb, Kenneth, and Hatry, Harry. Obtaining Citizen Feedback. URI 18000. Washington, D.C.: Urban Institute, 1971.

Weiss, Carol, and Hatry, Harry. An Introduction to Sample Surveys for Government Managers. URI 30003. Washington, D.C.: Urban Institute, 1971.

Winkel, Gary. "Community Response to the Design Features of Roads, A Technique for Measurement." Highway Research Record, No. 305. Washington, D.C.: Federal Highway Research Administration, 1970.

Legal Background

"A Bibliography of Periodical Literature Relating to the Law of Historic Preservation." Law and Contemporary Problems, vol. XXXVI, no. 3 (Summer 1971): 442-444.

"Aesthetic Nuisance: An Emerging Cause of Action." New York University Law Review, (November 1970).

Agnor, William. "Beauty Begins a Comeback: Aesthetic Considerations in Zoning." Journal of Public Law. vol. II (1962): pp. 260-284.

Anderson, Frederick R. NEPA in the Courts: A Legal Analysis of the National Environmental Policy Act. Washington, D.C.: Resources for the Future, 1973.

Ashmanskus, Donald. "Design and Site Review Boards: Aesthetic Controls in Local Governments." Management Information Service Report, vol. 7, no. 7, part B. Washington, D.C.: International City Management Association, February 1975.

Baldwin, Malcolm. "Historic Preservation in the Context of Environmental Law: Mutual Interest in Amenity." Law and Contemporary Problems: Historic Preservation, vol. XXXVL, no. 3 (Summer 1971): 432-441.

Broughton, Robert, "Aesthetics and Environmental Law: Decisions and Values." Land and Water Review, vol. VII (1972).

California Environmental Quality Act: California Publishing Res. Code, Sec. 21000 et. seq. (1970).

Christensen, K., et. al. "State-Required Impact Evaluations of Land Developments: An Initial Look at Current Practices and Key Issues." Working Paper 0214-01. Washington, D.C.: Urban Institute, July 1974.

Leighton. "Aesthetics as a Legal Basis for Environmental Control." Wayne Law Review, July-August 1971.

Lindbloom, Carl. Environmental Design Review. Technical Guide Services. West Trenton, New Jersey: Chandler Davis Publishing, 1970.

Mandel, Michael. "The Various Legal Frameworks for Utilizing Impact Measures in Land Use Decision-Making." Washington, D.C.: Urban Institute, forthcoming.

Minano, Dennis. "Aesthetic Zoning: Creation of a New Standard." Journal of Urban Law, vol. 48, no. 3 (April 1971).

Montana Environmental Quality Council. Second Annual Report. Helena, Montana, October 1973.

Montgomery County Maryland Planning Board. Everything You Always Wanted to Know About... Planning, Zoning, and Subdivision in Montgomery County, Maryland. (October 1973).

National Trust for Historic Preservation, with the Advisory Council on Historic Preservation and Legislative Reference Section of the Library of Congress. Guide to Federal Programs Related to Historic Preservation. Washington, D.C.: National Trust for Historic Preservation, 1973.

New York City Urban Design Council. Housing Quality: A Program for Zoning Reform. New York; 1972 or 1973.

Searles, Sidney Z. "Aesthetics in the Law." New York State Bar Journal, vol. 41 (April 1969) 210-217.

Wilson, Paul E., and Winkler, H. James. "The Response of State Legislation to Historic Preservation." Law and Contemporary Problems, vol. XXXVI, no. 3 (Summer 1971): 330-347.

Related Reading

Barry, Brian, and Horton, Frank. Geographic Perspectives on Urban Systems with Integrated Readings. Englewood Cliffs, New Jersey: Prentice Hall, Inc., 1970.

Blair, Louis, and Schartz, Alfred. How Clean Is Our City? Washington, D.C.: Urban Institute, 1972.

Dewey, Richard, "Peripheral Expansion of Milwaukee County." American Journal of Sociology, 1949.

Gelwicks, L. E. "Home Range and the Use of Space by an Aging Population," in Spatial Behavior of Older People, ed. by Leon Pastalan and Daniel H. Carson. Ann Arbor, Michigan. Institute of Gerontology, University of Michigan, 1970.

Great Britain, Department of the Environment. Guide to the Legislation in the Listing of Historic Buildings. London: Department of the Environment, 1969.

Gutman, Robert. "Site Planning and Social Behaviors." Journal of Social Issues, vol. XXII, no. 4 (1966).

Hurlbert, Randall L. "Noise Control: A Basic Program for Local Governments." Management Information Service Report. vol. 7, no. 3. Washington, D.C.: International City Management Association, March 1957.

Keyes, Dale. Land Development and the Natural Environment: Estimating Impacts. Washington, D.C.: The Urban Institute, forthcoming.

Kryter, Karl. The Effects of Noise on Man. New York: Academic Books, 1970.

Ladd, William. "Residential Location and Shopping Patterns." Paper. Ann Arbor, Michigan: University of Michigan, December 1966.

Langford, M. Community Aspects of Housing for the Aged. Ithaca, New York: Center for Housing and Environmental Studies, University of Pennsylvania, 1966.

Lynch, Kevin. Image of the City. Cambridge, Massachusetts: MIT Press, 1960.

Michelson, William. Man and His Urban Environment: A Sociological Approach. Reading, Massachusetts: Addison - Wesley Publishing Company.

Muller, Thomas. Fiscal Impacts of Land Development: A Critique of Methods and Review of Issues. URI 98000. Washington, D.C.: Urban Institute, 1975.

_____. Economic Impacts of Land Development. Washington, D.C.: Urban Institute, forthcoming.

Niebanck, P.L. The Elderly in Older Urban Areas. Institute for Studies, University of Pennsylvania, 1965.

Regnier, V.A. Neighborhood Cognition of Elderly Residents, Exchange Bibliography, #393. Council of Planning Librarians, April 1973.

Schaenman, P., Keyes, D., and Christensen, K. Estimating the Impacts of Land Developments on Selected Services. Washington, D.C.: Urban Institute, forthcoming.

Schaenman, P. and Muller, T. Measuring Impacts of Land Developments: An
     Initial Approach URI 86000. Washington, D.C.: Urban Institute,
     November 1974.

Schulz-Norberg, Christian. Existence, Space and Architecture. New York:
     Praeger Publishers, 1971.

Westin, A. Privacy and Freedom. New York: Athenium Press, 1970.

Wilson, Robert L. "Livability of the City: Attitudes and Urban Development"
     In Urban Growth Dynamics in a Regional Cluster of Cities, ed. by F.
     Stuart Chapin and Shirley Weiss. New York: Wiley and Sons, Inc., 1962.

APPENDIX—SAMPLE CITIZEN SURVEY

OBJECTIVE OF SURVEY

This is an example of a survey that can be used in collecting baseline data on current citizen uses and perceptions of their neighborhood. The survey was developed as part of this report. It has had only limited pre-testing and has not been tried out by a local government. The questions on the survey may serve as prototypes for quickie surveys (several questions geared toward one specific impact area) or for multi-purpose comprehensive surveys (questions geared to several impact areas). The survey includes questions related to the seven impact areas: recreation patterns at public facilities; recreational use of informal outdoor spaces; shopping opportunities; pedestrian dependency and mobility; perceived quality of the natural environment; personal safety and privacy; and aesthetic and cultural values. Questions on the socio-economic characteristics of the respondent are also included.

Before using this survey, staff members should clearly determine the objectives of their study, choose the appropriate impact areas and questions to be covered, and then pretest those questions to ensure that they are relevant to both the people being surveyed and the objectives of the study.

Our pretests indicate an average survey duration of about 35 to 45 minutes. The length varies with the number of household members and the extent to which open-end questions are answered.

OVERVIEW OF SURVEY QUESTIONS

VARIABLES	APPROPRIATE QUESTIONS
Interview	
Interview Numbers	1
Interviewer Number	2
Street Block	3
Neighborhood Code	4
Length of Interview	60
Household Characteristics	
Number in household by age and sex	16
Number of years in home	55
Number of years in neighborhood	56
Type of dwelling	61
Number of automobiles	53
Physical disabilities	54
Income	58
Race	59
Recreation Patterns: Uses and Perceptions (public facilities)	
Facilities used by household	17
Ages of users for each facility	16
Frequency of use for each facility	18
Usual mode of transportation to facility	19
Additional type of facilities desired	22
Factors affecting nonuse of facilities	21
Overall satisfaction with public recreation opportunities in neighborhood	20

VARIABLES	APPROPRIATE QUESTIONS
Recreation Patterns: Uses and Perceptions (informal places)	
Childrens' outdoor play areas	
Type and location	27
Satisfaction	28
Factors affecting dissatisfaction	29
Identification of undesirable play areas	30
Adult gathering places	
Satisfaction	31
Factors affecting dissatisfaction	32
Shopping Patterns and Preferences	
Facilities (identified by type, location or grouping) used by household	37
Frequency of use for each facility or group of facilities	38
Usual mode of transportation	39
Types of additional stores preferred for the area	40
Types of stores unwanted in the area	41
Perceived desirability of nightclubs and bars for the area	42
Satisfaction with location of grocery stores	43
Factors affecting dissatisfaction	44
School	
Satisfaction with location of elementary schools	23
Factors affecting dissatisfaction	24

VARIABLES	APPROPRIATE QUESTIONS
Pedestrian Dependency and Mobility	
Number of automobiles per household	53
Number of households relying on walking mobility to:	
Stores	39
Recreation facilities	19
Mass transit	
Satisfaction with availability of mass transit (bus service)	25
Factors affecting dissatisfaction	26
Perceptions of Environmental Quality	
Noise	
Indoor satisfaction with outside noise levels	47
Factors affecting dissatisfaction	48
Air quality	
Satisfaction	45
Factors affecting dissatisfaction	46
Personal Safety and Welfare	
Perceived safety at night	34
Safety from traffic	29, 21
Privacy	
Satisfaction with privacy in exterior spaces (i.e., yards or balconies--when appropriate)	35
Factors affecting dissatisfaction	36

VARIABLES	APPROPRIATE QUESTIONS
Perceptions of Neighborhood Aesthetics	
Rating of overall attractiveness	8
Identification of visually attractive places or features	11, 12
Identification of ugly or unattractive places or features	9, 10
Views	
Satisfaction with view from home	13
Factors affecting dissatisfaction	14
Landscaping characteristics	
Satisfaction	15
Maintenance and upkeep	
Streets and sidewalks	5
Yards	6
Exteriors of buildings	7
Overall Satisfaction with Neighborhood	49
Perceived neighborhood improvements	50
Identification of unique places in neighborhood	51, 52
Data for Future Surveys	
Definition of perceived neighborhood boundaries (areas people relate to strongly)	33

SURVEY INSTRUMENT

1. Interview number   _____

2. Interviewer number   _____

3. Street block   _____

    Time interview began   _____

Hello, my name is _____. I work with the city planning

department of _____. | offer identification card |

We are trying to make each neighborhood in the city better for the people who live

there. You can help by telling us what you like or dislike about your neighborhood,

and what you think should be done to make your neighborhood a better place to live.

Your opinions will be used in our planning efforts and will be kept strictly confi-

dential. None of your neighbors or anyone else will know what you have said. If

you wish to make sure that this a real survey please call the city planning

department. The number is on this card.

| have night and day telephone numbers on the card |

| if the respondent is too busy to talk say |

We would really like to get your opinions. May I please come back when you have

more time?

| if yes, say |

What time would be most convenient for you? | record time | _____

| if respondent refuses interview at any time, conclude the interview by saying: |

Thank you.

| proceed as instructed in training period |

if respondent agrees to interview, continue

First, I need to know:

Do you live in this house?   yes_____   no_____

if there is doubt that the respondent is over 18 years of age, ask

Are you 18 years or older?   yes_____   no_____

if respondent is under 18 years or not a member of this household, say

Is the head of the household or some other adult member of the household at home?

                              yes_____   no_____

if there is not an available adult ask what would be a good time to call back
and conclude the interview, say _____

                    Thank you.   record time to call back_____

leave an identification card indicating when you will call back

proceed as instructed in training period

Prior to administering the survey, the planning department will define the boundaries of neighborhoods included in the survey.   The boundaries will be identified
in the following question. Boundaries are often defined as a function of census
tracts; man-made or natural boundaries --e.g. railroad tracks or mountains--schools
or health delivery areas, or by combinations of the above. When possible the boundaries should be recognizable to most of the respondents.

4. Many of the questions I will ask you refer to places or conditions in your

    neighborhood. When I use the word neighborhood, I mean the area that extends

    from _____on one side   to _____

    _____: _____ and to

    _____ on the other three sides.

    Neighborhood code _____

Okay, here is the first question I'd like to ask you circle response

5. How satisfied are you with the cleanliness of the street and sidewalks in your

   neighborhood? Are you very satisfied, satisfied, dissatisfied, or very dissatisfied?

| VERY DISSATISFIED 1 | DISSATISFIED 2 | SATISFIED 3 | VERY SATISFIED 4 | don't care 5 | don't know/ no response M |

	Col	Code

6. How satisfied are you with the cleanliness of neighborhood yards? Are you very satisfied, satisfied, dissatisfied, or very dissatisfied?

[circle response]

VERY DISSATISFIED	DISSATISFIED	SATISFIED	VERY SATISFIED	don't care	don't know/ no response
1	2	3	4	5	M

7. How satisfied are you with how the outsides of the buildings are kept up?

[circle response]

VERY DISSATISFIED	DISSATISFIED	SATISFIED	VERY SATISFIED	don't care	don't know/ no response
1	2	3	4	5	M

8. Now, I would like to ask you some questions about how attractive you feel this neighborhood is. First, do you feel that it looks very attractive, fairly attractive, fairly unattractive, or very unattractive?

[circle response]

VERY UNATTRACTIVE	FAIRLY UNATTRACTIVE	FAIRLY ATTRACTIVE	VERY ATTRACTIVE	don't care	don't know/ no response
1	2	3	4	5	M

9. When you think about how your neighborhood looks, are there any particular buildings or places that look especially ugly or unattractive?

[circle response]   1. yes   2. no   M. don't know/ no response

go to Q 10   go to Q 11

10. Could you tell me which buildings or places those are?

During pretesting   record their responses. after their last response, draw a line and ask: Are there any others? (Ed.) this will allow you to prompt fuller answers but still indicate which ones came spontaneously from the respondent.

Are there any others?
1.
2.
3.
4.
5.
6.
7.
8.
9.
M. don't know/no response

11. Are there any specific places, buildings, or features that you think are

    especially attractive?

    | circle response | 1. yes   2. no   M. don't know/
                                                                no response

                            | |
                            ↓   ↓
                    | go to Q 12 | | go to Q 13 |

12. Could you tell me which things they are? | if not volunteered |

    | During pretesting record their responses. After their last response
    draw line and ask |
                            ↓
    Are there any others?

    1.
    2.
    3.
    4.
    5.
    6.
    7.
    M. don't know/no response

13. How satisfied are you with the view from your home? Are you very satis-

    fied; satisfied; dissatisfied; or very dissatisfied?

    | | | | VERY | don't | don't know/
    | VERY | | | SATISFIED | care | no response
    | DISSATISFIED | DISSATISFIED | SATISFIED | SATISFIED | |
    | 1 | 2 | 3 | 4 | 5 | M

                    | |
                    ↓   ↓
            | go to Q 14 | | go to Q 15 |

14. Why do you say that?

    | Do not read responses. During pretesting record the responses they
    give. After the last answer draw a line and ask |

    Are there any other reasons: ←

    1.
    2.
    3.
    4.
    5.
    6.
    7.
    8.
    M. don't know/no response

	Col	Code

15. How satisfied are you with the landscaping, trees, shrubbery, and grass

in the neighborhood? Are you very satisfied, satisfied, dissatisfied, or

very dissatisfied? [circle response]

VERY DISSATISFIED 1	DISSATISFIED 2	SATISFIED 3	VERY SATISFIED 4	don't care 5	don't know/ no response M

Could you please tell me how many people live in this home?

[record number] _____

M = don't know
     no response

For our planning purposes it is important to know the ages and sexes of the

people now living in this neighborhood.

16. Could you please tell me the age and sex of each other person who regularly

lives here. Please start with the oldest person and give me the letter on

this card. That shows their age group and please identify their sex.

[record this information on the following sheet]

[printed card will not have option M]

less than 5 yrs. A	6-12 yrs. B	13-18 yrs. C	19-34 D	35-49 E	50-64 F	65 and over G	dont know/ no response M

[use the spread sheet for recording the responses to Q 16-Q 19]

17,18,19 [Introduction to Questions 17,18,19 is on this page. Questions on next]
Now I would like to ask you about the neighborhood places members of your

household use for recreation. Let's consider such places as public parks,

playgrounds, and swimming pools that are near your home.

RECREATION PATTERNS

16.

17. Prior to the interview, the facilities will be listed by name below. Starting with respondent ask:

Do you or does (household members by age or role, e.g., husband, child, if obvious) EVER USE (name of facility)?

M = don't know/no response

18. ANSWERS
number of times

per month	per week
1. 1-3	1
2. 4-8	1-2
3. 9-16	3-4
4. 17-24	5-6
5. 25 or more	daily
M. don't know/ no response	

QUESTIONS

About how many times a week or a month does (household member) use this facility   circle code

19. ANSWERS
Means of transportation

1. walking
2. bike
3. car
4. bus
5. other
M. don't know/no response

QUESTIONS

What means of transportation does he (or she) usually use to go there   circle code

AGE record age code

SEX circle answer

1. Male
2. Female

Facilities to be inserted by city

	Q17	Q18	Q19
Person 1.			
a.	1. yes 2. no M	1 2 3 4 5 M	1 2 3 4 5 M
b.	1. yes 2. no M	1 2 3 4 5 M	1 2 3 4 5 M
c.	1. yes 2. no M	1 2 3 4 5 M	1 2 3 4 5 M
d.	1. yes 2. no M	1 2 3 4 5 M	1 2 3 4 5 M
e.	1. yes 2. no M	1 2 3 4 5 M	1 2 3 4 5 M
Person 2.			
a.	1. yes 2. no M	1 2 3 4 5 M	1 2 3 4 5 M
b.	1. yes 2. no M	1 2 3 4 5 M	1 2 3 4 5 M
c.	1. yes 2. no M	1 2 3 4 5 M	1 2 3 4 5 M
d.	1. yes 2. no M	1 2 3 4 5 M	1 2 3 4 5 M
e.	1. yes 2. no M	1 2 3 4 5 M	1 2 3 4 5 M

Person 3.

1. Male
2. Female

a.	1. yes	2. no	M	1 2 3 4 5 M	1 2 3 4 5 M
b.	1. yes	2. no	M	1 2 3 4 5 M	1 2 3 4 5 M
c.	1. yes	2. no	M	1 2 3 4 5 M	1 2 3 4 5 M
d.	1. yes	2. no	M	1 2 3 4 5 M	1 2 3 4 5 M
e.	1. yes	2. no	M	1 2 3 4 5 M	1 2 3 4 5 M

Person 4.

1. Male
2. Female

a.	1. yes	2. no	M	1 2 3 4 5 M	1 2 3 4 5 M
b.	1. yes	2. no	M	1 2 3 4 5 M	1 2 3 4 5 M
c.	1. yes	2. no	M	1 2 3 4 5 M	1 2 3 4 5 M
d.	1. yes	2. no	M	1 2 3 4 5 M	1 2 3 4 5 M
e.	1. yes	2. no	M	1 2 3 4 5 M	1 2 3 4 5 M

Person 5.

1. Male
2. Female

a.	1. yes	2. no	M	1 2 3 4 5 M	1 2 3 4 5 M
b.	1. yes	2. no	M	1 2 3 4 5 M	1 2 3 4 5 M
c.	1. yes	2. no	M	1 2 3 4 5 M	1 2 3 4 5 M
d.	1. yes	2. no	M	1 2 3 4 5 M	1 2 3 4 5 M
e.	1. yes	2. no	M	1 2 3 4 5 M	1 2 3 4 5 M

Person 6.

1. Male
2. Female

a.	1. yes	2. no	M	1 2 3 4 5 M	1 2 3 4 5 M
b.	1. yes	2. no	M	1 2 3 4 5 M	1 2 3 4 5 M
c.	1. yes	2. no	M	1 2 3 4 5 M	1 2 3 4 5 M
d.	1. yes	2. no	M	1 2 3 4 5 M	1 2 3 4 5 M
e.	1. yes	2. no	M	1 2 3 4 5 M	1 2 3 4 5 M

Col   Code

20. Taking everything into consideration, how satisfied are you with the public recreation opportunities in your neighborhood? Are you very satisifed, satisfied, dissatisfied, or very dissatisfied?

| circle response |

VERY DISSATISFIED	DISSATISFIED	SATISFIED	VERY SATISFIED	don't care	don't know no response
1	2	3	4	5	M

21. Are there any special reasons why members of your household do not use neighborhood public recreation facilities more than they do?

| do not read responses; circle the most appropriate reasons |

- 00. no reason
- 01. poor health
- 02. age (too old or young)
- 03. threat of danger from other people at or en route to the facility
- 04. threat of physical danger from facility equipment or setting
- 05. distance to the facility from the home
- 06. lack of supervision for children
- 07. dangerous traffic condition (en route to facility)
- 08. use of private facilities
- 09. wrong types of equipment or facility (i.e, activity)
- 10. other _____
- MM. don't know/no response

22. What, if any, type of recreation facilities do you feel are needed in your neighborhood, in addition to what is there now?

| do not read responses; circle the ones they mention |

- 0. none
- 1. swimming pools
- 2. tennis courts
- 3. basketball courts
- 4. baseball diamonds
- 5. playgrounds for children
- 6. parks
- 7. horseback riding stables
- 8. other (specify) _____
- M. don't know/no response

23. How satisfied are you with the location of the elementary schools in the neighborhood? Are you very satisfied, satisfied, dissatisfied, or very dissatisfied? | circle response |

VERY DISSATISFIED	DISSATISFIED	SATISFIED	VERY SATISFIED	don't care	don't know/ response
1	2	3	4	5	M
go to Q 24			go to Q 25		

Col   Code

24. Why do you say that?

┌───┐
│ do not read responses, circle the ones that come closest to their answers │
└───┘

   1. the schools are not within walking distance for my children
   2. the schools are too near my home; too noisy
   3. the schools are too near my home; kids trespass on my property,
       scare me, threaten me
   4. too much vehicle traffic on the routes to walk to school
   5. environment around school is too noisy
   6. environment around school is too bad for kids - whores, pornography
   7. other (specify) _____
   M. don't know/no response

25. How satisfied are you with the public bus service near your home?
    Are you very satisfied, satisfied, dissatisfied, or very dissatisfied?

VERY DISSATISFIED	DISSATISFIED	SATISFIED	VERY SATISFIED	dont care	don't know no response
1	2	3	4	5	M

            ↓   ↓
           │go to Q 26│   │go to Q 27│

26. Why do you say that?

┌──┐
│ do not read responses, circle the ones that come closest to their │
│ answers.   │
└──┘

   1. buses do not run frequently enough (if mentioned specify the time of
       day and day of week when buses do not run frequently enough) _____

   2. buses don't go to right destinations (specify the places missed
       _____
   3. bus stop is too far from my home
   4. fare too high
   5. poor waiting conditions
   6. buses too hot or cold
   7. prefer car _____(detail reason if possible)
   8. buses too dirty
   9. other (specify)_____
   M. don't know/no response

	Col	Code

Now, I would like to ask you some questions about how your children and other members of your family use the neighborhood streets, yards, sidewalks, and open areas for recreation.

> ask Q 27-30 only if there are children under 18 years old in the household.

27. Throughout the year, what are the outdoor places in your neighborhood where the children or teenagers in this family usually play?

> do not read responses; check the places and ask the approximate locations; circle location response.

<table>
<tr><td></td><td></td><td>location</td><td></td></tr>
<tr><td>1. private yards</td><td>1. yes 2. no</td><td>_____</td><td>1. on same side of block</td></tr>
<tr><td>2. sidewalks</td><td>1. yes 2. no</td><td>_____</td><td></td></tr>
<tr><td>3. streets</td><td>1. yes 2. no</td><td>_____</td><td>2. across the street on same block</td></tr>
<tr><td>4. parks</td><td>1. yes 2. no</td><td>_____</td><td></td></tr>
<tr><td>5. open lots</td><td>1. yes 2. no</td><td>_____</td><td>3. within 2-4 blocks</td></tr>
<tr><td>6. school yards</td><td>1. yes 2. no</td><td>_____</td><td>4. over 4 blocks</td></tr>
<tr><td>7. other_____</td><td>1. yes 2. no</td><td>_____</td><td>M. don't know/no response/not specified</td></tr>
<tr><td>M. don't know/no response</td><td></td><td></td><td></td></tr>
</table>

28. How satisfied are you with the outdoor play areas for children? Are you very satisfied, satisfied, dissatisfied, very dissatisfied?

VERY DISSATISFIED	DISSATISFIED	SATISFIED	VERY SATISFIED	dont care	don't know/ no response
1	2	3	4	5	M

go to Q29 and 30   go to Q31

29. Why do you say that?

> do not read responses, circle the ones that are closest to their answers.

01. not enough places -- existing places too crowded
02. not enough variety
03. too much automobile traffic for the children's safety
04. the places are too far from home
05. not enough playground equipment for the children
06. there are undesirable kids who hang around the areas
07. the children play too close to my home
08. debris and garbage near play area
09. deep water near play area
10. drunk people/bars near play area
11. dangerous machinery/structure
12. drug usage/sales
13. other_____
MM. don't know/no response

30. Where are the places that have that problem?

     1.
     2.
     3.
     4.
     5.
     6.
     7.
     8.
     M. don't know/no response

31. How satisfied are you with the places outdoors that you can use to sit
     and talk with friends? Are you very satisfied, satisfied, dissatis-
     fied, or very dissatisfied?

VERY DISSATISFIED	DISSATISFIED	SATISFIED	VERY SATISFIED	dont care	don't know/ no response
1	2	3	4	5	M

          go to Q 32   go to Q 33

32. Why do you say that?

     do not read responses; circle the answers that come closest to their
     answers

     1. there are no places to use
     2. they are too noisy
     3. they are too crowded
     4. there are no benches
     5. other (specify)_____
     M. don't know/no response

33. What parts of this area do you consider to be your own personal terri-
     tory--the places you most strongly identify with? Please be as specific
     as possible.

     If possible,give them base maps of the area, and on acetate overlays
     have them mark the boundaries. This may be difficult to do with the
     elderly and others.

     record response here   code here

                              1. confined to home
                              2. one block face
                              3. block and cross streets
                              4. 2-10 blocks or block faces
                              5. more than 10 blocks
                                  (linear or square)

Col   Code

Col   Code

34. How safe do you feel walking alone at night in your neighborhood?

		circle response			
VERY UNSAFE	FAIRLY UNSAFE	FAIRLY SAFE	VERY SAFE	don't care	don't know/ no response
1	2	3	4	5	M

35. | when appropriate | How satisfied are you with privacy available to you when you are in the yard around your home? | say "balcony" for apartment house when such space is available |

VERY DISSATISFIED	DISSATISFIED	SATISFIED	VERY SATISFIED	don't care	don't know/ no response
1	2	3	4	5	M

| go to Q 36 | | go to Q 37 |

36. What seems to be the problem?

| do not read responses, circle answers that come closest to theirs |

1. others can <u>see</u> into my yard from other buildings
2. others can <u>hear</u> us when they are outdoors in the own yards
3. too may **people** on the streets to feel any privacy outdoors
4. other_____
M. don't know/no response

Col.   Code

Now I would like to ask you about the neighborhood stores that members of your family may use for shopping purposes. I am going to read a list of different groups of stores in your area. Please tell me if you or members of your family ever use them.

prior to interview, the stores will be listed below by type and location. ask:

Per Month
1. 1 - 3
2. 4 - 8
3. 9 - 16
4. 17 - 24
5. 25 or more
M. know/no response

Per Week
1. 1
2. 1 - 2
3. 3 - 4
4. 5 - 6
5. daily or more
M. know/no response

1. walking
2. bike
3. car
4. bus
5. other
M. don't know/no response

37. Do any members of your household ever shop at:

38. On the average how many times a month or a week do any of you go there?

circle appropriate answer code; code is listed above

39. What means of transportation is usually used to go there?

(location/type of store or store group)

	37.	38.	39.
(location/type of store or store group)	M 1. No 2. Yes ——> don't know/no response	1 2 3 4 5 M	1 2 3 4 5 M
(location/type of store or store group)	M 1. No 2. Yes ——> don't know/no response	1 2 3 4 5 M	1 2 3 4 5 M
(location/type of store or store group)	M 1. No 2. Yes ——> don't know/no response	1 2 3 4 5 M	1 2 3 4 5 M
(location/type of store or store group)	M 1. No 2. Yes ——> don't know/no response	1 2 3 4 5 M	1 2 3 4 5 M

Col.   Code

40. What additional types of stores, if any, are needed within easy walking
distance or within a 5-minute drive from your home?

> do not read responses, circle answers that come closest to theirs

1. no others
2. all types or a variety of types
3. grocery stores
4. dry cleaners
5. pharmacies
6. other (specify) _____
M. don't know/no response

41. Are there any types of stores that you would prefer not to have in your
neighborhood?   circle response

1. no all stores are fine; can't think of any I would not want
2. yes department stores
3. yes liquor stores
4. yes laundromats
5. other (specify) _____
M. don't know/no response

42. Do you agree or disagree with this statement?

It is all right to have bars and nightclubs in my neighborhood. Do you
strongly agree, slightly agree, slightly disagree, or strongly disagree?

STRONGLY DISAGREE	SLIGHTLY DISAGREE	SLIGHTLY AGREE	STRONGLY AGREE	don't care	don't know/ no response
1	2	3	4	5	M

circle response

43. How satisfied are you with the locations of the grocery stores? Are you
very satisfied, satisfied, dissatisfied, or very dissatisfied?

circle response

VERY DISSATISFIED	DISSATISFIED	SATISFIED	VERY SATISFIED	don't care	don't know/ no response
1	2	3	4	5	M

Go to Q 44   Go to Q 45

44. Why do you say that?

> do not read responses, circle answers that come closest
> to theirs

1. too far away
2. bus service inadequate
3. in a bad or dangerous part of the neighborhood
4. it is dangerous to go there because of traffic
5. poor quality store; high prices; poor variety; wrong product
6. other (specify) _____
M. don't know/no response

45. When you are outdoors, how satisfied are you with the freshness and
cleanliness of the air? Are you very satisfied, satisfied, dissatisfied,
or very dissatisfied? circle response

VERY DISSATISFIED	DISSATISFIED	SATISFIED	VERY SATISFIED	don't care	don't know/ no response
1	2	3	4	5	M

Go to Q 46   Go to Q 47

46. Why do you say that?

> do not read responses, circle answers that comes closest to theirs.

1. the air is often smoggy
2. there are obnoxious **odors** (specify source, if mentioned   Ask where
     they come from, if not mentioned) _____
3. the air is filled with automobile exhaust fumes
4. the air is smoky (specify source, if mentioned)_____
5. other (specify)_____
M. don't know/ no response

47. When you are indoors how satisfied are you with the level of street noise
from cars, trucks, or people? circle response

VERY DISSATISFIED	DISSATISFIED	SATISFIED	VERY SATISFIED	don't care	don't know/ no response
1	2	3	4	5	M

Go to Q 48   Go to Q 49

48. Why do you say that?

| do not read responses, circle answers that come closest to theirs |

1. too noisy at night because of cars or trucks
2. too many trucks
3. the people at (specify)_____are too noisy
    (e.g., school, swimming pools)
4. industrial sounds are too loud (specify source, if mentioned)
5. construction sound (specify source, if mentioned)
6. neighborhood children too loud and noisy
7. I won't stay outdoors because it's so noisy
8. other (specify)
M. don't know/ no response

49. Taking everything into consideration, how do you presently feel about

living in this neighborhood? Are you very satisfied, satisfied, dissatis-

fied, or very dissatisfied? | circle response |

VERY DISSATISFIED	DISSATISFIED	SATISFIED	VERY SATISFIED	don't care	don't know/ no response
1	2	3	4	5	M

50. If you could advise the city of (_____) about needed

improvements in your neighborhood, what would you suggest?

| do not read responses; circle answers that are closest to theirs. through pretesting list the types of answers that most frequently appear. |

1.
2.
3.
4.
5.
6.
7.
8.
M. don't know/no response

51. If there would be change to your neighborhood, are there specific

places or parts that you consider to be special or unique, in other

words, things that you would not want changed or removed?

    1. Yes   2. No   M. don't know/no response

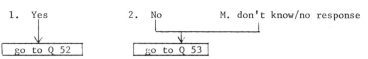

    go to Q 52   go to Q 53

52. What are these places or things?

> through pretesting identify those places or types of places, do
> not read responses; circle answers that come closest to theirs

1.
2.
3.
4.
5.
6.
7.
8.
M. don't know/no response

53. Now we would like to get a little background information on your family.

How many cars does your household own?

    record number of cars   _____

54. Is there anyone in the household who is physically disabled?

    1. Yes   2. No   M. don't know/no response

55. How many years have you or your family lived in this home?

    Record number of years
    or
    M. don't know/no response   _____

Col.	Code

56. How many years have you lived in this neighborhood?

> record number of years ____
> or
> M. don't know/no response

57. Do the people who live here own or do they rent this house (or apartment)?

     1. Own   2. Rent   M. Don't know/no response

58. In this survey of the neighborhood, we are trying to get a general picture of people's financial situation. Taking into consideration all sources of income, what was your total family or household income before taxes in 197_?   Please just give me the letter on the card.

> show printed card -- printed card will not have M on it.

	Per Year	Per Month	Per Week
E.	Less than $5,999	$333 - 499	$77 - 115
F.	$6,000 - 9,999	$500 - 833	$116 - 192
G.	$10,000 - 14,999	$834 - 1,249	$193 - 288
H.	$15,000 - 19,999	$1,250 - 1,666	$289 - 384
I.	$20,000 - 24,999	$1,667 - 2,083	$385 - 480
J.	Over $25,000	Over $2,084	Over $481
M.	Don't know/no response		

	Col.	Code

59. Could you also please tell me your race? Please give me the number appropriate from this card.

show card with printed choices ; circle their response

      1. Black

      2. Caucasian

      3. American Indian

      4. Chicano

      5. Oriental

      6. Other (specify) _____

      M. Don't know/no response

I have no more questions. Thank you very much for your help.

      Stopping time _____

60. Length of interview _____

61. Interviewer code

Type of dwelling: circle type

    1. Single-family home (detached)

    2. Single-family home (attached --townhouse or rowhouse)

    3. Multi-family highrise (X or more stories, multi-family)

    4. Garden apartments, low rise (2 to (X-1); multi-family units

SUMMARY A - PREFERRED NEIGHBORHOOD IMPACT MEASURES

1. Changes in socioeconomic, demographic characteristics of the population.

2. Change in number or percentage of households satisfied with recreation opportunities at public facilities.

3. Change in number or percentage of households satisfied with recreation in informal spaces around the home.

4. Change in number or percentage of households satisfied with shopping opportunities in the neighborhood.

5. Change in number or percentage of households satisfied with mass transit opportunities.

6. Change in number or percentage of households satisfied with location of schools.

7. Change in number or percentage of households satisfied with walking conditions in neighborhood.

8. Change in number or percentage of households satisfied with walking accessibility to destination.

9. Change in number or percentage of households satisfied with air quality.

10. Change in number or percentage of households satisfied with noise levels.

11. Change in number or percentage of households satisfied with personal security from traffic.

12. Change in number or percentage of households satisfied with personal security from crime.

13. Number of children physically at risk from unusual hazards (other than crime or traffic).

14. Change in number or percentage of households satisfied with privacy in outdoor areas around the home.

15. Change in number or percentage of households satisfied with the physical attractiveness of the neighborhood.

16. Change in number or percentage of households satisfied with view opportunities.

17. Number and type of cultural, historical or scientific landmarks to be lost or made inaccessible or accessible.

18. Change in number or percentage of households satisfied with their neighborhood.

19. Change in social interaction patterns.

LAND USE
USE LAND
LAND USE
USE LAND
LAND USE
USE LAND
LAND USE
USE LAND
LAND USE